CONCISE COLLEGE TEXTS

PATENTS, TRADE MARKS, COPYRIGHT AND INDUSTRIAL DESIGNS

OTHER BOOKS IN THIS SERIES
Tort, by C. D. Baker
The Making of Business Contracts, by A. Harding Boulton
Constitutional and Administrative Law, by H. W. Clarke
Contract, by F. R. Davies
Sale of Goods and Consumer Credit, by A. P. Dobson
Labour Law, by C. D. Drake
The English Legal System, by K. J. Eddey
Hotel and Catering Law, by David Field
The Law of Arbitration, by William H. Gill
Family Law, by Judge Brian Grant
Land Law, by E. Swinfen Green and H. Henderson
ONC/OND Commercial Law, by C. Hamblin and F. B. Wright
Advanced Level Law, by Barry Jones
British Government Today, by Barry Jones
Estate Duty in England and Wales, by A. Douglas Lawton
  (Adapted from *An Outline of Estate Duty in Scotland* by
  G. Herbert Brown and John M. Halliday)
Landlord and Tenant, by J. R. Lewis and J. A. Holland
General Principles of Law, by C. L. Newton
Equity and Succession, by Roger Samuels
Construction Law, by John Uff
Solicitor's Introduction to Accounts, by D. B. Williams and M. A. Stein

AUSTRALIA
The Law Book Company Ltd.
Sydney : Melbourne : Brisbane

CANADA AND U.S.A.
The Carswell Company Ltd.
Agincourt, Ontario

INDIA
N. M. Tripathi Private Ltd.
Bombay

ISRAEL
Steimatzky's Agency Ltd.
Jerusalem : Tel Aviv : Haifa

MALAYSIA : SINGAPORE : BRUNEI
Malayan Law Journal (Pte.) Ltd.
Singapore

NEW ZEALAND
Sweet and Maxwell (N.Z.) Ltd.
Wellington

PAKISTAN
Pakistan Law House
Karachi

CONCISE COLLEGE TEXTS

PATENTS, TRADE MARKS, COPYRIGHT AND INDUSTRIAL DESIGNS

SECOND EDITION

BY

T. A. BLANCO WHITE
One of Her Majesty's Counsel

ROBIN JACOB
Barrister-at-Law

AND

JEREMY D. DAVIES
Barrister-at-Law

LONDON
SWEET & MAXWELL LIMITED
1978

First Edition, 1970

Second Edition, 1978

*Published in 1978 by
Sweet and Maxwell Limited of
11 New Fetter Lane, London,
and printed in Great Britain
by The Eastern Press Ltd. of
London and Reading.*

ISBN *Hardback* 0 421 24090 3
Paperback 0 421 22890 3

©
T. A. Blanco White, Robin Jacob and Jeremy D. Davies
1978

PREFACE TO THE SECOND EDITION

A lot has happened, in the field covered by this book, since the last edition, and much has had to be re-written. The main change is in the law of patents, where the Patents Act 1977 has changed almost everything. Here, a warning is called for. Our publishers felt that this book would be more use if it was produced at once, as soon as the new Patents Act was passed, than if we waited to see how the thing developed. So we have had to do quite a lot of guessing. We guessed that the Act would actually come into force on January 1, 1978: it now looks like June (or August) and when we refer to "old" patents, we mean patents applied for before that date. We have had to guess what some of the Rules under the Act will say. Above all, we have had to guess what the new Act means: it is an almost unbelievably badly constructed Act, and time and again poses problems for the reader, as to what if anything those responsible were trying to say, that only years of judicial decisions can settle. In bigger books than this, it is possible to explain the difficulties and discuss the various possible meanings; we have had to guess what the courts were likely to say. Broadly speaking, though, this little book should not be far wrong.

We hope this book will be published before the new Patents Act comes into force. Nevertheless, we have written it as if the new law were already applied, with notes (mostly at the ends of chapters) as to differences in the law as it now stands. What is more, we had actually to write it before the last lot of amendments had been made; and not everything amended could be changed in proof. The following points call for comment here:

1. References throughout to " the end of 1977 " or " the beginning of 1978 " should now be read as referring to the date some time in mid-1978 when the new Act comes into force. This applies particularly to pages 17, 18, 30 and 52.

2. The old British law of infringement will apply to acts done before that date and may apply to all infringements of " old " patents before or after that date; not only in cases started before then, as stated on page 18.

3. There are no longer any grounds of invalidity which affect

Preface

existing disputes only (see p. 29). In addition, certain grounds of invalidity, which were to have been abolished entirely, and were therefore not mentioned in this work, are now to be retained for " old " patents only. The most significant of these are:

(1) *Inutility*: that the invention does not do what the patentee says it will.
(2) *No fair basis*: that the claims are not supported by the description, and especially that they are too wide.
(3) *False suggestion*: that the application or the specification contained a false statement on some essential point.
(4) *Not best method*: that the patentee failed to disclose the best method known to him of working the invention.

There are other grounds which are of negligible practical importance.

4. Not all existing patents are extended to 20 years (p. 30). The transitional provisions separate existing patents into two categories: " New existing patents " are those which were granted less than 11 years before the appointed day (since about mid-1967); these are automatically extended to 20 years. " Old existing patents," granted before mid-1967, will expire after 16 years, but may be extended for up to four years on the ground that the patentee ought to have made more out of them than he has. If the application for extension is made before the new Act comes into force, an extension of up to 10 years is possible.

5. The new rule in relation to the costs of an action for a declaration of non-infringement (p. 51) may or may not apply to actions relating to old patents. The same applies to the rule that a threat against a manufacturer is not actionable.

T. A. B. W.
R. J.
J. D. D.

The Temple,
November, 1977

CONTENTS

	Page
Preface to the Second Edition	v
Table of Cases	xi

I. INTRODUCTION

1. IMITATIONS AND REMEDIES 1
    Imitations 1
    Remedies 3
    Foreign Law 7
        Note: Compensation for Infringement . . 8

2. PATENT, COPYRIGHT OR DESIGN? 11
    Patents 11
    Copyright and Industrial Designs . . . 12
    Periods of Protection 13
    " Imitations " and Copying 14

II. IMITATING THE PRODUCT

3. PATENTS AND HOW TO GET THEM 16
    Three New Systems of Patent Law . . . 16
    Who Applies 18
    The Specification and the Claims . . . 18
    Securing Priority 20
    Patentability 21
    Delay in Application 22
    Examination Procedure 23
    Grant of the Patent 23
    Cost and Period of Protection 24
    Grant and Ownership 25
    Patent Agents 25
        Note: The Grounds upon which a Patent may be Declared Invalid . . 25
        Note: The Old Application Procedure . 27
        Note: Inventions by Employees . . 27
        Note: Sources of the Law . . . 28
        Note: Security Restrictions. . . . 29

4. HOW MUCH USE ARE PATENTS? 30
    The Importance of Validity 30
    Evading Patents 30
    Licensing 32

vii

Contents

	Page
5. PATENTING IMPORTANT INVENTIONS	34
Introduction	34
Where Others have Tried	34
An Important Invention	35
The Action for Infringement	41
Threats	42
Misuse of Patents	43
"Improvement" Patents	43
Taxation and Patents	44
Note: Patenting Drugs and Similar Chemical Compounds	45
Note: The Definition of Infringement	46
Note: The "Old" Law	47
6. INDUSTRIAL DESIGNS	48
Introduction	48
Consequences of 1968 Act	48
The Present Law	49
The Copyright Work	49
"Reproduction"	50
Who may be Sued	51
Care of Copyrights	52
Designs that are Registered	52
7. CROWN RIGHTS AND SECURITY	53
The Crown's Right to Work Patents	53
Keeping Inventions Secret	54

III. TRADE MARKS AND UNFAIR COMPETITION

	Page
8. DIFFERENT DEGREES OF PROTECTION	55
Passing-off	55
Passing-off and Registration of Trade Marks	56
"Part A" and "Part B" Marks	57
Litigation Caused by Uncertainty	58
Protection under the Criminal Law	59
9. WHAT REGISTERED TRADE MARKS ARE FOR	60
Introduction	60
The Goods for which the Mark is Registered	60
Infringement	61
Exceptions to the General Infringement Rules	64
Who should be Sued for Infringement	66
Contested Actions	66
Special Rules for "Part B" Marks	66
Note: Tests for Infringement	67

Contents

		Page
10.	How to Register a Trade Mark	68
	Introduction	68
	What is a " Mark "?	68
	Registrable Marks	68
	The Application	71
	More about Oppositions	75
	Registration in Cases where Confusion is Likely	78
	More about Confusion	78
	Removal from the Register	79
	Defensive Registration of Trade Marks	80
	" Part B " Marks	81
11.	Pitfalls in Trade Mark Law	83
	Introduction	83
	The Old Rule—The Mark must not Mislead	83
	Changing the Way the Mark is Used	84
	Change in Ownership	84
	Split Ownership	85
	Parallel Imports	86
	Licensing of Trade Marks	86
	Marks that are the Name of the Article	88
	Non-Use	89
	The Need for Vigilance	90
	Foreign Marks	91
	The " Electrix " Story	92
12.	Certification Trade Marks	94
	The Nature of Certification Trade Marks	94
	Application	94
	Infringement	95
	Other Features of the System	95
13.	The Law of Passing-off	97
	A General Rule	97
	Varieties of Passing-off	97
	" Badges " and Reputations	97
	Odd and Unusual Instances	101
	Suing for Passing-off	103
14.	Slander of Goods	105
	The General Rule	105
	Examples	105
	Conclusion	106
15.	The Criminal Law	108
	Introduction	108
	The Trade Descriptions Acts 1968-72	108
	Conclusion	111

Contents

IV. COPYRIGHT

		Page
16.	**INTRODUCTION TO COPYRIGHT**	112
	Introduction	112
	The Nature of Copyright	112
	Copyright, Reputations and Competition	113
	Types of Copyright Dispute	114
	Copyright in Practice	114
	Copyright and Confidence	114
	Old Copyrights	115
	"Reproduction"	115
17.	**WORKS THE SUBJECT OF COPYRIGHT**	117
	"Works"	117
	Copyright can Exist only in "Works"	122
	Illegal and Immoral Works	123
	Overlapping Copyrights	123
	The Period of Copyright	125
18.	**THE OWNERSHIP OF COPYRIGHT**	126
	Introduction	126
	The Basic Rule—Copyright Belongs to the Author	126
	Crown Copyright	130
	Where Authorship is not Certain	130
19.	**WHAT IS INFRINGEMENT?**	132
	Introduction	132
	Infringement by Reproduction	132
	Other forms of Infringement	138
	Note: "Works"	144
20.	**WHAT IS NOT INFRINGEMENT**	148
	The Owner of the Copyright cannot Control Legitimate Copies	148
	Specific Exceptions to the Rules for Infringement	149
	The Right to Reproduce, subject to Royalties	151
21.	**DEALINGS IN COPYRIGHT**	152
	Introduction	152
	Formal Problems	152
	Contracts relating to Copyrights	155
	Taxation and Authors	160
22.	**CONFIDENCE AND COPYRIGHT**	162
	Introduction	162
	The Action for Breach of Confidence	162
	Sales of "Know-How"	169
	The Need for Agreements	170
	Difficult Cases	170
	Index	173

TABLE OF CASES

PAGE

ACKROYDS (London) *v.* Islington Plastics [1962] R.P.C. 97 164
" Aertex " Trade Mark. *See* Cellular Clothing Co. *v.* White.
Argyll (Duchess) *v.* Argyll (Duke) [1967] Ch. 302; [1965] 2 W.L.R. 790; [1965] 1 All E.R. 611 .... 164, 167
Argyllshire Weavers *v.* Macauley (Tweeds) Ltd. *See* " Harris Tweed."
Aristoc *v.* Rysta Ltd. [1945] A.C. 68; 62 R.P.C. 65 .... 63, 69

" BALI " Trade Mark. *See* Berlei (U.K.) *v.* Bali Brassiere Co.
Bass, Ratcliffe & Gretton Ltd. *v.* Nicholson & Sons Ltd. (" Triangle " case) [1932] A.C. 130; 49 R.P.C. 88 78
Berlei (U.K.) *v.* Bali Brassiere Co. [1969] 1 W.L.R. 1306; 113 S.J. 720; [1969] 2 All E.R. 812 76
Bismag Ltd. *v.* Amblins (Chemists) Ltd. (1940) 57 R.P.C. 209 .. 63
Blacklock *v.* Pearson [1915] 2 Ch. 376 135
Bollinger *v.* Costa Brava Wine Co. (" Spanish Champagne ") [1960] Ch. 262; [1959] 3 W.L.R. 966; [1960] R.P.C. 16; [1959] 3 All E.R. 800 101
―― *v.* ―― [1961] 1 W.L.R. 277; [1961] R.P.C. 116; [1961] 1 All E.R. 561 59
Boots' Trade Mark (1937) 54 R.P.C. 327 70
British Northrop *v.* Texteam Blackburn [1973] F.S.R. 241; [1974] R.P.C. 57 .... 50, 118
Broad & Co. Ltd. *v.* Graham Building Supplies Ltd. [1969] R.P.C. 286 .... 57, 67

CELLULAR Clothing Co. *v.* White (" Aertex " Trade Mark) (1953) 70 R.P.C. 9 101
Centrafarm BV *v.* Winthrop BV (No. 16/74) [1976] 1 C.M.L.R. 1; [1976] F.S.R. 164 86
Coats (J. & P.) Ltd.'s Application (1936) 53 R.P.C. 355; [1936] 2 All E.R. 975 70
Coco *v.* A. N. Clark (Engineers) Ltd. [1969] R.P.C. 41 .. 163, 166, 167
Columbia Gramophone Co.'s Trade Marks (1932) 49 R.P.C. 239 90
Cow (P. B.) & Co. *v.* Cannon Rubber Manufacturers [1959] R.P.C. 347 52
Crosfield's Application (" Perfection " Trade Mark) [1910] 1 Ch. 130; 26 R.P.C. 854 69
Cummins *v.* Bond [1927] 1 Ch. 167 124

" DAIQUIRI RUM " Trade Mark [1969] F.S.R. 89 .... 60, 88
Davis *v.* Sussex Rubber Co. [1927] 2 Ch. 345; 44 R.P.C. 412 .. 81
Darling *v.* Honnor Marine [1965] Ch. 1; [1964] 2 W.L.R. 195; [1964] R.P.C. 160; [1964] 1 All E.R. 241 51
De Beers Abrasive Products *v.* International General Electric Co. of New York [1975] 1 W.L.R. 972; 119 S.J. 439; [1975] 2 All E.R. 599; [1975] F.S.R. 323 105
Dunlop Rubber Co.'s Application (" Trakgrip " Trade Mark) (1942) 59 R.P.C. 134 70

xi

Table of Cases

	PAGE
EASTEX Manufacturing Co.'s Application (1947) 64 R.P.C. 142; [1947] 2 All E.R. 55	81
Edge (William) & Sons Ltd. *v.* William Niccolls & Sons Ltd. [1911] A.C. 693; 80 L.J.Ch. 744; 105 L.T. 459; 27 T.L.R. 555; 55 S.J. 737; 28 R.P.C. 582	57
Edwards' Application (1946) 63 R.P.C. 19	77
Electrix *v.* Electrolux (Electrix Ltd.'s Application) [1960] A.C. 722; [1959] 3 W.L.R. 503; [1959] R.P.C. 283; [1959] 3 All E.R. 170	69, 71, 93
Electrolux Ltd. *v.* Electrix Ltd. (1953) 71 R.P.C. 23	93
EMI Records *v.* CBS Schallplatten GmbH [1976] 1 C.M.L.R. 75	86
FERODO Ltd.'s Application (1945) 62 R.P.C. 111	80
Francis Day & Hunter *v.* Bron [1963] Ch. 587; [1963] 2 W.L.R. 868; [1963] 2 All E.R. 16	134
Fraser *v.* Evans [1969] 1 Q.B. 349; [1968] 3 W.L.R. 1172; [1969] 1 All E.R. 8	169
GENERAL Electric Co. (of U.S.A.) *v.* General Electric Co. (" G.E." Trade Mark) [1972] 1 W.L.R. 729; 116 S.J. 412; [1972] 2 All E.R. 507; [1973] R.P.C. 297	79, 84
Greers Ltd. *v.* Pearman & Corder Ltd. (1922) 39 R.P.C. 406	105
" HARRIS TWEED " (Argyllshire Weavers *v.* A. Macauley (Tweeds) Ltd.) [1964] R.P.C. 477	101
Hayward & Co. *v.* Hayward & Sons (1887) 34 Ch.D. 198	106
Henriksen *v.* Tallon [1965] R.P.C. 434	19
Hensher (George) *v.* Restawile Upholstery (Lancs.) [1976] A.C. 64; [1974] 2 W.L.R. 700; 118 S.J. 329; [1974] 2 All E.R. 420; [1974] F.S.R. 173; [1975] R.P.C. 31	50, 118
INITIAL Towel Services *v.* Putterill [1968] 1 Q.B. 396; [1967] 3 W.L.R. 1032; [1967] 3 All E.R. 145	168
JACQUES & Sons Ltd. *v.* Chess (1940) 57 R.P.C. 77	101
Jellinek's Application (" Panda " Trade Mark) (1946) 63 R.P.C. 59	77
KAT *v.* Diment [1951] 1 K.B. 34; 67 R.P.C. 158; [1950] 1 All E.R. 657	109
Kingston-upon-Thames Royal London Borough *v.* Woolworth (F. W.) & Co. [1968] 1 Q.B. 802; [1968] 2 W.L.R. 223; [1968] 1 All E.R. 401	108
" Kojak " case. *See* Tavener Rutledge *v.* Trexapalm.	
MCCULLOCH *v.* Lewis A. May (" Uncle Mac ") (1947) 65 R.P.C. 58; [1947] 2 All E.R. 845	102
McDowell's Application (" Nujol " Trade Mark) [1927] A.C. 632; 44 R.P.C. 335	75
Mentmore *v.* Fomento (1955) 72 R.P.C. 157	106
Moorhouse and Angus & Robertson (Publishers) Pty. *v.* University of New South Wales [1976] R.P.C. 151	142
NO-NAIL Cases Pty. Ltd. *v.* No-Nail Boxes Ltd. [1946] A.C. 447; 63 R.P.C. 44	53
" Nujol " Trade Mark. *See* McDowell's Application.	

Table of Cases

	PAGE
" ORLWOOLA " Trade Marks [1910] Ch. 130; 26 R.P.C. 850 ..	79
" Ovax " Trade Mark. *See* Smith, Mayden & Co.'s Application.	
" PANDA " Trade Mark. *See* Jellinek's Application.	
Parker-Knoll *v.* Knoll International [1962] R.P.C. 265	100
Peacey *v.* De Vries (1921) Mac.C.C. (1917–23) 259	135
Phonographic Performance *v.* Pontin's [1968] Ch. 290; [1967] 3 W.L.R. 1622; [1967] 3 All E.R. 736	146
Procea *v.* Evans (1951) 68 R.P.C. 210	97
Pullman (R. & J.) Ltd. *v.* Pullman (1919) 36 R.P.C. 240	57, 103
RALEIGH Cycle Co. *v.* H. Miller & Co. [1951] A.C. 278; 67 R.P.C. 226; *see also* (1949) 66 R.P.C. 23	40
Reddaway (F.) & Co.'s Application [1914] 1 Ch. 856	68
Riding *v.* Smith (1876) L.R. 1 Ex.D. 91	106
Robb *v.* Green [1895] 2 Q.B. 315	165
SALTMAN Engineering Co. *v.* Campbell Engineering Co. (1948) 65 R.P.C. 203; [1963] 3 All E.R. 413n.................	163
Seager *v.* Copydex [1967] 1 W.L.R. 923; [1967] R.P.C. 349; [1967] 2 All E.R. 415	163, 166
" Sherry " case. *See* Vine Products *v.* MacKenzie.	
Shredded Wheat Co. *v.* Kellogg Co. (1940) 57 R.P.C. 137	88
Sirdar's Agreement [1975] 1 C.M.L.R. D93; [1975] F.S.R. 492, EC Commission Decision	86
Smith, Hayden & Co.'s Application (" Ovax " case) (1946) 63 R.P.C. 97	75, 76, 77
Smith Kline & French Laboratories' Application [1974] F.S.R. 106	68
" Spanish Champagne." *See* Bollinger *v.* Costa Brava Wine Co.	
" Stilton " Trade Mark [1967] R.P.C. 173	95
TAVENER Rutledge *v.* Trexapalm (" Kojak " case) (1975) 119 S.J. 792; [1975] F.S.R. 479	102
" Trakgrip " Trade Mark. *See* Dunlop Rubber Co.'s Application.	
" Triangle " case. *See* Bass & Co. *v.* Nicholson & Sons.	
" UNCLE MAC." *See* McCulloch *v.* Lewis A. May.	
VANE *v.* Famous Players Film Co. (1928) Mac.C.C. (1923–28) 347	139
Vine Products *v.* MacKenzie (" Sherry " case) [1969] R.P.C. 1	101
WALKER *v.* British Picker Co. (1961) R.P.C. 57	118
Weiss's Patents (1949) 66 R.P.C. 281	40
Westinghouse *v.* The Varsity Eliminator Co. (1935) 52 R.P.C. 295	64
White Hudson & Co. *v.* Asian Organisation [1964] 1 W.L.R. 1466; [1965] R.P.C. 45; [1965] 1 All E.R. 1040	99
Wombles *v.* Wombles Skips [1975] F.S.R. 488	102
Wright's case (Wright, Layman & Umney *v.* Wright) (1949) 66 R.P.C. 149	100
YORKSHIRE Copper Work's Application [1954] 1 W.L.R. 554; 71 R.P.C. 150; [1954] 1 All E.R. 570	69

PART I

INTRODUCTION

1

IMITATIONS AND REMEDIES

IMITATIONS

THE subject of this book is the law of commercial and industrial imitation: imitation by one manufacturer of another's products, imitation by one trader of the names and badges by which another's goods or business are known.

Overlap of the types of imitation

In law, these two varieties of imitation are best treated as distinct; in practice, they overlap. For one thing, the imitation of a rival manufacturer's goods often depends for its profitability on being able to tell customers that this is an imitation of something they will have heard of; people are usually willing to pay more for products they have heard of. For another, where imitation of goods is close enough for the imitation to look like the original, the similarity of appearance is usually itself enough to suggest to customers knowing the one product that the other is really the same thing. Again, in these days of advertising, it is often more important that a product should be convincingly advertised than that it should work well; and it may be that the main reason for wanting a product to be different from its rivals is to make it easier to advertise that product as being different.

The commercial use of legal rights

One result of this sort of overlap is that the various legal rights with which this book is concerned are by no means always used for the purposes that the law supposes them to serve. In legal theory, a patent—and much of this book is concerned with patents—should normally be reckoned as valueless unless it enables its owner to secure an order from the courts forbidding a competitor to make or sell something that competitor would otherwise want to put on the market.

Introduction

To some businesses, that is indeed the purpose of patents. To others, however, the mere possession of a patent, however rubbishy to the lawyer's mind, may be of real value for advertising purposes. Others again treat patents merely as cards in complicated games of business politics that no lawyer understands. Industrial designs, on the other hand, are given protection, in theory, to protect the work of the designer—to protect the artistic element in manufacture. In many cases, however, the main value of design protection is to supplement the manufacturer's trade marks by securing to him exclusive rights in the "get-up" of his goods—a function that, in legal theory, belongs rather to the law of passing-off. Again: copyright is mainly concerned with the way ideas are expressed and its primary function is to enable authors, composers and so on to make some sort of living from their work—to protect a special sort of product of a special sort of manufacturer. But industrial designs are very often closely related to copyright works—drawings or models—so that copyrights are likely to be the main obstacles to the copying of an industrial design. There is a special registration system for industrial designs, but it is not much used, and we shall not devote much space to it. (Parliament has unfortunately called the right given by registration of an industrial design " copyright " too, but to avoid confusion we shall use the word " copyright " for copyright proper only: *i.e.* for the rights given under the Copyright Act 1956.) In addition, such things as the instruction leaflet for a new gadget are usually copyright, and these copyrights are sometimes important.

The scheme of this book

For reasons of convenience in exposition, this book is divided into sections broadly along the lines drawn by the Acts of Parliament dealing with these branches of the law. The basic division is into three parts: the first part is concerned with the copying of the product and deals mainly with the law of patents and of industrial designs; the second part is concerned with the way things are sold and deals mainly with the law of passing-off, trade marks and other rules preventing unfair competition or unfair selling techniques; and the third part deals with the law of copyright (apart from its use to protect industrial designs) and the law of confidential information.

Enough has been said, however, to make it clear that the division is merely a matter of convenience; any commercial problem must be treated as a whole, and commercial disputes often enough cut across these lines. It is indeed one of the functions of a book of this sort to show the inter-relations between these different subjects, in a way that more specialised works cannot easily do.

REMEDIES

"Exclusive rights"

Most of the legal rights with which this book is concerned are rights to stop other people doing things. For some reason, Acts of Parliament do not put it like that: thus the proprietor of a registered industrial design is said by the Act to have " the exclusive right " to do certain things with the design, and the other rights here concerned are expressed in similar language. But what is meant is, not that the owner of the design, or patent, or copyright concerned has by that ownership the right to do anything he could not otherwise do, but that he has the right—subject to questions of validity—to decide whether other people shall be permitted to do certain things or not. This point is worth emphasising, because the position is too often not understood. In particular, many if not most of the people who take the trouble to secure patents for inventions believe that, somehow, possession of the patent secures to them the right to manufacture their inventions without interference. It does nothing of the sort: the thing such an inventor wants to manufacture may well incorporate other people's patented inventions, and the only way the inventor can be sure that he has the right to manufacture is by searching to find what patents other people have. His own patent gives him (if it is valid, and his specification is properly drawn up—points discussed later in this book) the right to stop other people using the particular device that is the subject of the patent—and gives him nothing else. In principle, the position is much the same with the other rights considered in this book, although ownership of a registered trade mark, exceptionally, gives a limited freedom from infringement of other people's trade marks.

Other rights

This book also deals with certain rights which are rather different from the above described rights to stop infringement: in particular it deals with forms of passing-off and the like which are different in nature; and it deals also with certain other parts of the law—such as the prevention of the misuse of confidential information and the action to

Introduction

prevent threats of patent litigation. By and large, what is said below about litigation applies in these cases too, although prosecutions to prevent and punish the use of false trade descriptions are different because such use is criminal in nature.

Infringement

Since most of the various rights here discussed are similar in nature, they are enforced in essentially the same way —by an action in the courts (in England, normally in the High Court) for "infringement" of the right. The real point of most such actions is, that in this law-abiding country, once the owner of the right has made it clear that he insists on his right, and once the court has declared that the right exists, few business men will want to argue the point any further. Although the owner of the right usually asks for, and usually gets (if he wins his action) an injunction against further infringement—a formal order, that is, from the court to the infringer, forbidding infringement for the future—it is the decision that really matters, not the formal order. Indeed, such an order is so rarely disobeyed in commercial cases (where the defendant is almost always a company) that no really effective method of dealing with real disobedience has ever been worked out. In practice the thing to do against individuals who are determined infringers is to sue not only any companies which are controlled by them which are infringing for the time being, but also the individuals themselves. This prevents these individuals from forming new companies for the purpose of infringing—disobedience of an injunction by an individual means, ultimately, imprisonment.

When to sue

Such an action for infringement can be brought either when infringement has already started, or at an earlier stage, when infringement is threatened; in general, the law allows one whose rights are infringed to choose when to sue. If infringement has already taken place, a successful plaintiff will be entitled to damages for what has already occurred as well as to an order for the future, and to an order that any goods or materials whose use would infringe his rights be delivered up to him or rendered innocuous. In many cases, he can instead of damages claim to have paid over to him the profits the infringer has made from his infringement. However, litigation in England is expensive, and although the losing party will be ordered to pay the winner's costs, the amount paid will fall well short of covering the bills the winner will have to pay. Even if damages are reckoned in with the costs the loser pays, there is very, very seldom money to be made by this sort of litigation. Actions are brought to punish the infringer, to stop further infringement by him or others, to establish the legal position for the future; very seldom should they be brought for the sake of the damages. It follows that, in almost all cases, the right time to start an action for infringement (if an action is to be started at all) is when infringement first starts—or even better, when infringement is first threatened. This is especially true of actions for infringements of trade mark and of actions to stop passing-off, since in these cases the right to sue may be lost by delay.

There are other reasons why actions for infringement are best brought quickly if they are to be brought at all. The best way to win an action is not to have to fight it; so that the best sort of action to start is the sort that will not be defended. Whether an action is defended or not naturally depends in large degree on whether the case is important enough to the defendant to make it worth while going to the trouble and expense of fighting—and facing the uncertainty of not knowing what the result will be. The defendant in an infringement action faces the prospect of an injunction against continuing to do business in the way he has been, and it is not easy to plan ahead not knowing whether such an injunction will be issued or not. Accordingly, just as few people start infringement actions unless they feel they must, so few people defend them unless they feel they must. If an infringer is allowed to infringe in peace for years—to spend money advertising a new trade mark or a new product; to develop a new market to the point where it becomes profitable, perhaps even to build a new factory or re-equip an old one—he may well feel that there is so much at stake that he must fight; yet if the action had been brought earlier on, before there was so much at stake, he would probably have dropped the thing and cut his losses rather than waste time and money fighting. There are always other products and other markets. In trade mark cases especially is this so: it is very, very rarely worth fighting for a new trade mark, even if the chances are in your favour.

Time and cost

Although the various rights with which this book is concerned are all enforced by actions of much the same nature,

Introduction

the cost and complexity of litigation varies widely between the different cases. Actions for infringement of patent are in a class by themselves: in complexity, in cost, in the time needed to bring them to trial. Few patent disputes are finally settled within three years; so that an infringement which will have ceased to be commercially important within three years or so is often hardly worth suing against at all, whilst an infringer who can be sure of stopping infringement within three years or so can often face the possibility of an action with comparative equanimity. This considerably reduces the practical value of British patents. A copyright, trade mark or passing-off action can be brought to trial in a matter of months, and the cost and trouble are much less, too. Actions for infringement of industrial designs are intermediate in character; whether they are more like patent actions or more like copyright actions depends on how the parties handle them.

Interlocutory injunctions

There are cases in which to wait a matter of months is to wait months too long. In these cases, the court may be asked to act at once, and to grant at the outset an injunction against infringement—not a permanent injunction, but an interlocutory one, lasting until the trial of the action. In particular, many trade mark infringements, many cases of passing-off (especially where there is a suggestion that the defendant is dishonest), and many infringements of copyright are best dealt with in this way. A plaintiff who is granted an interlocutory injunction must give what what is called a " cross-undertaking in damages ": that is, he must undertake that, if in the end his action fails, he will compensate the defendant for the interference to the defendant's business effected by the injunction. In most cases, this is not an important matter; but an interlocutory injunction in a patent case may well stop a production line, and the damage caused to the defendant may be very great. At the same time, the final result of the action is seldom entirely certain. So the risk to the plaintiff involved in asking for an interlocutory injunction may be too great and should be carefully considered before an application for an interlocutory injunction is made. Provided the plaintiff acts as soon as the infringement is brought to his notice—this is essential—an interlocutory injunction will often be granted by the court in order to preserve the status quo until the trial. Unless the evidence fails to disclose that the plaintiff

Imitations and Remedies

has any real prospect of success at the trial, the court will consider whether the balance of convenience lies in favour of granting or refusing an interlocutory injunction. An important consideration in weighing the balance of convenience is whether the plaintiff or the defendant will be adequately compensated in damages if an interlocutory injunction is either wrongfully refused or wrongfully granted.

Inspection and discovery orders

In the last few years, cases of piracy appear to have become much commoner in many different fields of commerce. Partly in response to this, the courts have held that in extreme cases, orders can be made upon the application of the plaintiff alone requiring the defendant to permit the plaintiff's solicitors to inspect his documents and premises immediately. The purpose of this is of course that an unscrupulous defendant is given no time to destroy incriminating documents or evidence. The courts have also held that even innocent persons who have become " mixed up " in the wrongdoing (*e.g.* the Customs, or innocent warehousemen and the like) can be compelled to disclose at least the name of the wrongdoer. Such persons (save, possibly, the Customs who are in a special position) can also be restrained from permitting pirate goods from leaving their possession until at least there has been time for the case to come properly before the court.

FOREIGN LAW

This is a book about English law. Almost all foreign legal systems have something corresponding more or less to the various rights discussed in this book, but the correspondence is seldom close. Commonwealth countries, and to some extent the United States too, have legal systems like ours; but their patent law is our old patent law, not our new one (see Chap. 3) and few of them have our use of copyright to control copying of manufactured goods. Other countries, including European countries, have basically different legal systems, so that even where their law is supposed to be the same as ours—as with the new European patent law, see Chapter 3—it is unlikely to work out in practice the same way as ours. Questions about the law of foreign countries should be put to foreign lawyers. But the law of the EEC is now part of our law, and we will have to try and understand it.

Introduction

NOTE: COMPENSATION FOR INFRINGEMENT

The usual procedure in any action for infringement is that the issue of liability is decided first: only if the plaintiff wins, does the issue of how much compensation the defendant must pay him, arise. The successful plaintiff has then a choice: to be compensated according to the damage the infringement has done to his own business, or, instead, to have paid over to him the profits made by the infringer from the infringement. In either case, only the damage suffered or profits made in the six years immediately prior to the issue of the writ in the action and since the issue of the writ can be awarded. In exceptional cases, where the court for some reason disapproves of the plaintiff's conduct, profits can be refused, but damages can be refused only in special cases discussed below. Of course, neither problem may arise in some cases—for example where the infringer merely made samples of an infringing article to see what would happen.

What happens in practice is this: the plaintiff makes his choice of damages or profits and the court orders a corresponding investigation. Before the investigation takes place (before, therefore, the plaintiff and defendant have seen each other's books) the infringer usually makes an offer (he may even have made this offer earlier, before the issue of liability was determined). If the plaintiff accepts, well and good; if the plaintiff refuses, the investigation takes place, but at the plaintiff's risk as to costs: if the amount found due is less than was offered the plaintiff pays for the investigation; if it is more the infringer pays. Normally, the infringer pays " into court " (into an official bank account) the amount offered.

(*a*) *Damages*

If the plaintiff elects to have damages the court orders an inquiry into just how and how much the infringement has injured the plaintiff. There is an exception to this, however, in the case of patents, designs and copyright where an infringer can escape the payment of damages if, at the time of the infringement, he was not aware, and had no reasonable grounds for supposing, that the monopoly infringed existed. (Such innocence is not uncommon in patent and design cases: it is rare in copyright cases, since most " works " of recent origin are pretty well bound to be copyright and the infringer who copies them ought to have known that. Note that in any case, the infringer who goes on infringing after warning can no longer be innocent.)

In copyright cases, the plaintiff can claim, additionally, damages not only for infringement, but also for conversion: that is, he can demand to be treated as the owner of all infringing copies of his work, and if the infringer or anyone else has disposed of any or destroyed them the plaintiff can claim damages for the loss of his property. It is this rule which enables

Imitations and Remedies

a copyright owner to obtain relief against a dealer in infringing copies of his work even where the dealer was not responsible for making the infringing copies and had ceased dealing with them. The rule is subject to the limitation that the plaintiff cannot get paid twice for the same lot of damage, once for infringement and again for conversion. In cases of infringement of copyright in industrial designs, conversion damages are unduly harsh: it is proposed that this remedy be abolished. Innocence (in the sense discussed above) will protect a seller of infringing copies from having to pay damages for conversion and so will ignorance that they were infringing copies, but he will have to deliver up any infringing copies still in his possession to the plaintiff. (Note that because of this special rule a copyright owner can demand that any infringing copies still in the infringer's possession be handed over *without* the usual option of rendering them innocuous.)

As to the measure of damages, the plaintiff is entitled to exact compensation for any monetary damage he has actually suffered that can be fairly attributed to the infringement. Thus, if an infringing book or machine has sales of so many, the author or inventor will have lost so many royalties. A plaintiff who is a manufacturer or publisher can ask the court to assume (unless the infringer can show that this was not so) that each infringing sale has cost him a sale, and so lost him the profit on a sale. There may be other heads too: the owner of a trade mark which is infringed may have to pay for additional advertising to restore the position; the owner of an infringed patent or design may be forced, whilst waiting for the action to be tried, to reduce profit margins in order to retain any share of the market. All that can go in. Or the matter may be approached in a different way: pirating of a copyright work may render the work valueless, or passing-off may partly or wholly destroy a goodwill. Damages may be assessed by estimating the value of the copyright before and after the infringement and taking the difference. Some cases are complicated of course; but it is seldom difficult to make a rough estimate of the sum likely to be involved. The key question, when dealing with a manufacturer-plaintiff, is: what is his profit on a sale?

(b) *Profits*

When it comes to taking an account of profits, it is the infringer's profits that matter, not the plaintiff's. They are harder to assess. For one thing, no court has ever asked the sort of question an accountant asks: such as the extent to which (in assessing the profit from infringement) that particular part of the business can properly be loaded with overheads, or even promotion expenses. In addition it is the profits from infringement that matter, and they may or may not be separable from other matters giving rise to profits. Suppose, for example, a book of which only part infringes; or a stocking, of which all that was

Introduction

patented was the way the toe was made. It may be very difficult to say what part of the profit is attributable to that. It is often even harder for a plaintiff to guess what the answer is going to be before he has seen the defendant's books. Accordingly, it is usually too risky to ask for an account of profits and it is seldom asked for in practice. Not always, however. Suppose that the inventor of the stocking toe can say: " Making the toe my way saves, on average, per dozen pairs of stockings, so many minutes of operative's time at so much an hour "—then an estimate of the profit from the invention is directly available for comparison with estimates of damages before the plaintiff makes his election.

In copyright cases innocence is no defence to a claim for profits. In other cases it probably usually is a defence.

2

PATENT, COPYRIGHT OR DESIGN?

IN considering protection of a new product against imitation, the first question is whether the case calls for patenting, can be left to copyright or is one of the special cases where design registration is advisable.

PATENTS

A patent is granted to protect an article that is essentially better in some way than what was made before, or for a better way of making it. The monopoly a patent gives can extend to any other improved article or process which is better for the same reasons as that on which the patent is based. In an extreme case, a patent can be wide enough and represent a big enough advance over earlier ideas to give its owner a complete monopoly of an industry. For instance, there have been patents giving for a time a monopoly of telephones, a monopoly of pneumatic tyres or a monopoly of transistors. Very few patents are as important as that, but the existence of almost any patent (if it is, or is thought to be, valid) will make it necessary for a competitor to do design work or even major research of his own rather than copy the actual product he wishes to imitate.

When patents suffice

Whether in a particular case the law of patents can give a manufacturer the protection he needs, depends mainly on three things: how new his product is, how important it is, and for how long he needs protection. The degree of novelty will decide whether he can get a patent, and if so how wide a monopoly this patent may be made to give him. The importance of the product will decide how much trouble it will be worth a competitor's taking to get over the monopoly and how big a risk of legal attack a competitor will be prepared to face. The time factor may decide whether it is practicable to carry out the design or research work needed to avoid a monopoly whose validity cannot safely be challenged.

If, then, a manufacturer needs freedom from competition while he builds up a new business of substantial size, only

Introduction

a patent of unusually wide scope with a really important invention behind it will do: any ordinary patent could be got over by competitors long before the business was firmly established. If what is wanted is a monopoly in a new line of goods not of great importance a patent of comparatively narrow scope should suffice, for it will usually be less trouble for competitors to produce something different than to risk trouble with patents. In intermediate cases it may be very hard to get proper protection: where goods are markedly more successful than what was made before without being very strikingly different, it is doubtful whether any patent can prevent imitation. This point is important and will be considered more fully in the course of the next two chapters.

COPYRIGHT AND INDUSTRIAL DESIGNS

Copyright

The external appearance of many, probably most, new industrial designs is covered by copyright, in the drawings or the model in which the design of that article first took shape. Where this is so, copying of the article will involve infringement of the copyright. There are no formalities and no fees: where copyrights exist they come into existence automatically when the design is created. Of course, a copyright in the design will not prevent others making and selling articles that are made or work in the same sort of way. But in some fields (many toys, for instance) the design really is the essence of the thing. Even where this is not so, a copyright covering the design can prevent exact copying.

One thing that copyright can do is to secure distinctiveness to goods that are better than their rivals by reason of better workmanship or some other difference of that sort which cannot itself be the subject of a legal monopoly. If it is possible to lead the public to associate the better quality with the new design, then copyright should give adequate protection.

Registration of designs

Where there is doubt whether a new product will be covered by copyright, protection for its design can often be secured by registration. This is none too cheap and must be done before the design is shown to anyone otherwise than in strictest confidence. But sometimes it should be worthwhile. In particular, the sort of design that someone else would be sure to come up with fairly soon may call for registration, to deal with competitors who reach the same design independently. A copyright is not infringed except by actual copying, but a registered design (if validly registered) is infringed by anyone using the same design even if he thought of it independently. Inevitably, though, it is much easier to persuade a court that someone else's design is the same as yours if you can show that he actually copied.

PERIODS OF PROTECTION

The periods of protection given by patents, copyrights and design registrations are all different.

(a) Patents

A patent lasts—so long as renewal fees are paid—for 16 or 20 years from the date when the full specification of the invention is filed at the Patent Office (this need not be the date of first application for a patent): for patents " dated " before mid-1967, 16 years with a possibility of extension to 20; for late ones, 20 years with no extensions. Patent protection, however, does not become fully effective until the specification is published by the Patent Office. This will always take a good many months from the date when the patent is applied for. The patenting of a quickly-produced and short lived line of goods may thus be completely useless: the patent may have lost its importance before it comes fully into force.

Of course the delay in publication may sometimes be an advantage for the invention can be kept secret until publication date.

(b) Copyright

Copyright in an artistic work arises when the work is made so that the owner of the copyright gets immediate protection and there is no period of waiting for registration. In general, the period of copyright is the life of the author plus 50 years, but use of a copyright work as an industrial design ceases to be an infringement 15 years after the date of first marketing of the product made to that design. The result is that new industrial designs are normally protected by copyright for much the same period as if they were newly patented or their designs were registered.

Introduction

(c) Registered designs

The registration procedure for a design may take two or three months, and until then there is no registration and no protection. (So, with articles that are very quick and easy to copy, such as most things moulded in plastics, registration ought to be applied for some three months before they are first shown to the trade, and then copying can be stopped at once.) The registration lasts for five years from the application, and can be kept alive on payment of further fees for two further five-year periods. Few design owners find this worth doing.

" IMITATIONS " AND COPYING

In an action for infringement of a patent or a design registration, it makes, in theory, no difference whether infringing goods are copied from those of the owner of the patent or design, or the makers of the infringements worked entirely on their own. In practice, a defendant who has copied is always more likely to lose the action; but in theory the only questions to be decided are first: whether the patent or design registration is a valid one; and, secondly, whether the monopoly given by it is wide enough to cover the alleged infringement. Even if the " infringer " did not know of the existence of the patent or registration concerned this will not make any difference to the giving of an injunction against him; nor even in most cases to his liability to pay damages and to pay the costs of the action. In an action based on copyright the position is different: the action will only succeed if it can be shown that the alleged infringement was copied (directly or indirectly) from the copyright work.

It follows that a new product, developed entirely by the staff of the company that makes it, may well be an infringement of patent or design rights belonging to a competitor. Throughout this book, when we speak of " imitations," we mean to include such independently developed products. In the case of designs, the risk is not usually very serious and can be easily avoided by a proper search. The risk of innocent infringement of patents, however, in any industry where there is appreciable technical progress, will usually be a serious one if the new product is noticeably different from the old. There is no way of avoiding this risk except thorough acquaintance with or thorough search of all existing patents in the branches of industry concerned; in fields such as electronics these may number thousands. No

Patent, Copyright or Design?

attempt is made in this book to suggest any other way, and discussions in later chapters on avoiding patents refer only to patents whose existence is already known. A thorough search of a field of any size is difficult and rather expensive; a good patent agent will do it as cheaply as it can be done.

The essence of a patent is that the inventor gets a monopoly in return for full disclosure of his invention in the specification which he files at the Patent Office and the Patent Office publishes. (These published specifications are an extremely valuable source of information in many fields; in some fields they are almost the only reliable source of information about recent developments.) Sometimes, however, technical knowledge is best protected by not publishing it at all. Even where an invention is patented, those who work it soon acquire special knowledge of how to work it. Such unpublished information is a sort of property, and the law will sometimes protect it. It is discussed in Chapter 22.

PART II

IMITATING THE PRODUCT

3

PATENTS AND HOW TO GET THEM

Three New Systems of Patent Law

Up to now, we have made do in this country with a single system of patent law that we have worked out for ourselves in the course of the last century or two. Things are now to be different: any patent applied for after mid-1978 will be governed by one of three new systems. There are to be EEC patents, with one set of rules; European patents that are not EEC patents, with another set of rules; and new British patents with a third. The three sets of new rules will bear a family resemblance to each other, but will not be the same. For " old " patents, on the other hand—patents already granted, or based on applications filed in 1977 or before—the old British system will carry on. For the next 20 years, then, we are going to have four different sorts of patent in force in this country. Furthermore, there are going to be two different ways of applying for one of the new British patents: applying here, or making an international application. (European and EEC patents will be issued not by our Patent Office at all, but by the European Patent Office being built in Munich.)

For most purposes of a simple book like this one, the distinctions between the different sorts of patent can be disregarded; but inevitably there are times when a lot depends on which sort of patent you are thinking of.

The EEC authorities are suspicious of things like national patents that may give a manufacturer in one part of the EEC the right to exclude goods made in other parts; so naturally the EEC patents are to be single patents for the whole EEC. Applications for them will be handled by the European Patent Office in Munich (if an application is made, say, in London, it will be handed on to Munich); and when they are granted they will be in force throughout the EEC. If such a patent is infringed here, the infringer will usually have to be sued in our courts; but only questions of infringement can be tried here, questions of validity can be raised only in Munich.

European patents will also be dealt with up to the granting of the patent by the Munich Office; but once they are granted, they will take effect as if they were a set of national patents, one for each of the countries the applicant "designated" in his application.

The next possibility is an international application for national patents: again, there is a single application, handled in its early stages by a single patent office (which may be the Munich Office, but could be one of a number of others, depending partly on the sort of industry involved) and there is to be only a single search to see how new the invention is; but after that, it will be treated as a set of applications for national patents for the various countries "designated" by the applicant, each national patent office making its own decision whether to grant a patent or not. Lastly, it will be possible just to apply to the British Patent Office for a United Kingdom patent only; but under the new procedure, which is like the European procedure rather than the procedure we are used to here.

The old British application procedure will continue to apply where a "complete specification" (see below) has been filed before mid-1978; it is described briefly in a Note at the end of this chapter. The old British law of infringement applies only to infringements started before mid-1978; the differences are small. As to the law of validity of patents, see the Note at the end of this chapter.

European or British

Which sort of patent, then, is it going to make better sense to ask for? This is a hard question to answer, until we know how well the European Patent Office in Munich is going to work. But some things are beginning to be clear. First, cost. The European patent is going to be expensive, by our standards; but if patents are wanted in more than one or two other European countries it may still be cheaper than a series of separate patents. (There seems little to choose, in cost, between EEC and European patents.) If there are to be patents in more than a very few foreign countries (in Europe or outside) an international application will save money. Next: possible delay. International application ought to be as quick in processing as national ones; but we do not yet know for certain, nor do we know how long

Imitating the Product

it may take to get European or EEC patents through to actual grant. Furthermore, a patent specification (see below) drawn up to suit the practice of one country will seldom be fully suited to others. International applications, even European applications, using a single specification for a whole series of countries, are not going to have the best possible specification everywhere. With EEC patents this will matter less (since validity of the patent will not be decided nationally) but the point may still be worth keeping in mind. As between EEC and European patents, one may guess that the EEC patent could be preferable.

There will certainly be cases where a British inventor ought to apply both for an EEC (or European) patent and for a British patent. In the first place, it looks as if British patnts would be obtainable for types of invention that the European Office would disallow: computer programmes, for instance: perhaps contraceptive techniques. (See below under "Patentability.") Secondly, the European Patent Office is likely to reject for obviousness inventions that would be patentable here. In such cases, it could make sense to apply for both in case the European Office rejected the application altogether.

Who Applies

The right to apply for a patent belongs to the owner of the invention—the inventor himself, or anyone who can claim the invention from him. Other people can join in the application.

Most inventions are made by employees, as part of their job: in such cases, the employer owns the invention (see Note at the end of this chapter) and can apply to patent it, although he needs the inventor's signature (unless the invention is a foreign one, and he is patenting it here under the International Convention mentioned below). Or the inventor can make the application (in which case he will be a sort of trustee of it for his employer); or they may both apply together (when the inventor will still be a sort of trustee of his half-share).

The Specification and the Claims

The applicant must file at the Patent Office a document called a specification. This must contain a description of the apparatus or process or article, or whatever is to be the subject of the patent. It must contain instructions which will enable a skilled man to work the process, or make the apparatus or article as the case may be. Most important of all it must contain what are called " claims ": that is, statements defining the precise scope of the rights of monopoly that the patent will give. There is only one way of finding out whether the owner of a patent can prevent the manufacture and sale of a particular imitation of his patented product, and that is by looking up his specification and seeing whether the words of the " claims " describe that imitation. Claims are usually written in special jargon (to make them as generalised as possible) and a good deal of practice is needed to understand exactly what they are saying.

The way we use claims is rather special to British law. Although nearly all foreign countries have claims in their patents, and on paper might seem to use them as we do, this is seldom so in practice. Thus the European rules for using claims seem to us to fit British practice well enough; but the Germans can say the same, and their approach is quite different from ours. Nor is American practice the same as ours.

An example

Henriksen v. *Tallon* (1965) illustrates both the technical jargon of patent claims and the sort of difficulties which can occur when attempts are made to find out the meaning of such claims.

The invention was concerned with ball-point pens. The original " Biro " pen used a narrow ink reservoir, narrow enough for the ink to be prevented by surface tension from dropping out when the pen was held point upwards. It worked, but the ink deteriorated badly in storage; the ink at the end of the column was in contact with the air and the air affected the ink. The Henriksen invention was to keep the air from the ink by putting a plug of oil or grease on the end of the ink column; as the ink was used the plug moved along after it. What was more, the inventor found that, if the plug was just stiff enough, it would hold the ink in, even with a wide (" jumbo ") ink reservoir. His specification claimed the wide reservoir and the stiff (" pasty ") plug; but the defendants did not use the wide reservoir although they did use a plug. So the argument turned on Claim 1, which read:

" 1. A fountain pen of the ball tip type, comprising a tubular ink reservoir provided at one end with a ball

Imitating the Product

tip and at the opposite end with an air inlet, in which there is disposed between the column of ink in the reservoir and the air inlet a liquid or viscous or paste-like mass which does not mix with the ink and forms a plug which moves with the surface of the ink column and prevents air from contacting the surface of the ink."

One difficulty in the case arose over the meaning of "prevents air from contacting the surface of the ink": the defendant's plug may have reduced the amount of air getting to the ink only by about half. It was not surprising, therefore, that the defendants argued that their pens did not fall within the words of (that is, did not "infringe") Claim 1. However, that depended upon the meaning to be given to the quoted words. The trial judge, in holding infringement, thought that they covered a case where a plug protected the ink from the effect of the air "to a very substantial extent," even though there were small holes in it. The House of Lords, on the other hand, held that "prevents" meant "prevents for all practical purposes" and that since the evidence was that the used plug was good enough for commercial purposes (the pens would last for a good number of years) the defendants infringed the claim.

Securing Priority

Preparation of a specification is usually a long job, and it is often important that the patent should be applied for at the earliest possible moment. But the Act allows the applicant to secure a right of priority by filing an informal application in the first place (here or abroad); he then has a year to prepare and make a proper application. So long as the invention is well enough described in the original application to "support" the claims of the final one, the novelty of his invention will be judged as of the earlier date. The original application can simply be dropped: but there are snags; see "Delay in application" below. If it is dropped, the only penalty for getting the original specification wrong is loss of priority. The specification of the application that is finally proceeded with, however, not only has to pass detailed scrutiny by expert examiners at the Patent Office but also must be proof against the destructive criticism of hostile lawyers and experts: for if the patent is ever the subject of legal proceedings, the wording of the specification will determine the validity and scope of the patent.

Just what is necessary for an earlier specification to "support" the claims of a later one is not clear; as usual in our new Patents Act, the draftsman has been careful not to use words that mean anything very definite, either to a lawyer or to anyone else.

PATENTABILITY

Not every bright idea is patentable. A patentable invention has to be "capable of industrial exploitation"—including exploitation in agriculture, but excluding plant or animal varieties and "essentially biological processes for the production of animals or plants." Microbiological processes, though, can be patented; they are rather important, since many antibiotics are made by fermentation as well as many drinks. Medical and veterinary treatments are not patentable; but drugs are (even if the materials used are old; see Note to Chap. 5).

There is also a list of matters excluded from patentability as being essentially intellectual: scientific theories; mathematical methods; computer programmes; aesthetic creations of all sorts. However, the British rule is that industrial techniques are patentable even if their only novelty lies in one of these excluded fields (which means that the exclusion can usually be dodged by clever wording); the European rule looks like being stricter, so ours may get changed. In the same way, British practice has been to allow patents for methods of contraception (as not being, strictly, medical treatment), but the European Office may think otherwise and our rule may then change. In any event, it always has been possible (and probably always will be) to get borderline applications allowed by wording them so that it does not occur to the Patent Office to raise this sort of objection. It is points like this that make the services of an experienced patent agent so valuable.

SEARCH, PUBLICATION, EXAMINATION

If it is intended to proceed with a patent application the next step is to request (and pay for) a preliminary examination and a search of earlier patents. The preliminary examination goes to the formal correctness of the appli-

Imitating the Product

cation and specification; the search, in the first place at least, will be through earlier published British specifications for the same sort of invention. At the same time, the application and its specification will be published, probably 18 months after filing. This means that if the inventor wants to avoid publication (as he may: see below, under "Delay in application") the application must be withdrawn.

The next stage is for the applicant to request (and, as usual, pay for) a full examination. Here the examiner considers whether what is claimed is the sort of thing that is patentable at all; whether the specification is clear and complete enough to enable a skilled reader to work the invention; and above all, whether when compared with what appears in earlier specifications the invention appears new and not obvious. It is reasonably easy to decide whether a supposed invention is new—the examiner has only to read the claims of the specification and look in the earlier documents for anything falling within those claims. Deciding whether an invention is obvious, on the other hand, is always difficult and with nothing to go by except what appears in patent specifications becomes almost impossible. Naturally, then, examination for obviousness produces some odd objections: the only thing an examiner can do is turn the application down and see whether the applicant's patent agent can produce a convincing answer to the objection.

When examining for obviousness, the examiner considers only earlier specifications already published at the date when the application was filed (or the date of an earlier application giving priority, if there is one). But in considering whether the invention is actually new, he must look also at specifications published later but already on file at that date: in relation to novelty only, these are treated as if already published. This makes things complicated, see below.

Delay in Application

If a reasonable specification was filed with the application for a patent (either the application actually proceeded with, or an earlier one made here or abroad—see above, "Successive applications"), nothing after that counts in deciding on the validity of the patent. This is the main reason for getting an application in as soon as enough is known about the invention for a specification to be drawn up. If there is delay, some competitor, here or abroad, working along the same sort of lines may in the meantime publish some description, or market something, or make some patent application, that will make it difficult or impossible to get a valid patent at all. Or the inventors themselves may let out enough information to invalidate their own patent: by samples shown to the trade, perhaps, or by some note in a trade journal.

That problem can (as has been explained) be dealt with by getting on file an informal patent application that is good enough to support the claims in a proper application filed in due course. But getting priority in this way will not stop a competitor working along similar lines—and it is remarkable how often competitors are found to have been working along similar lines—from getting his own patent. If a competitor has a patent covering the same thing, it may be impossible to work the invention without a licence from him. To invalidate rival patents, it is necessary either to have made the invention public or to have filed a patent application (in this country, or an international or European one "designating" this country) which is in due course published. But it will seldom be safe to allow publication of an application intended only to give priority: it might anticipate the inventor's own later application too. So: not only should the first, informal application be filed as soon as practicable, the formal application should be filed as soon as practicable too. It used under our old system to be standard practice, to let as long as possible go by between making the first application and filing the complete specification; now, that will often be a mistake.

Examination Procedure

If an examiner sees an objection to the specification or its claims (or considers the whole thing unpatentable) he writes to the applicant's patent agent stating his objection. The applicants must show that he is wrong, or alter their specification or claims, or abandon the application. (If he and the agent cannot agree, the matter will go to a Superintending Examiner, and if necessary the applicant can appeal from him to the Patents Court).

Grant of the Patent

If and when all objections have been overcome, the applicant must pay another fee, and the patent will then be

Imitating the Product

granted. Its owner may then start to sue in the High Court for any infringements that have occurred since that application was published. The patent may still be revoked, however, either by the Patents Court or by the Patent Office, if anyone can show (in effect) that it should not have been granted. (Such an attack on the patent is almost certain to be made if the patentee sues for infringement, as part of the defence to the action.) The grounds for revocation differ markedly as between old and new patents: see the Note at the end of this chapter. To attack a patent in the Patent Office will be much cheaper than attacking it in the court, mostly because of the different way in which the evidence is provided; but an attack in the Patent Office will often be less likely to succeed.

COST AND PERIOD OF PROTECTION

A patent granted in London covers the whole United Kingdom, and proceedings upon it may be brought in the English, Scottish or Northern Irish courts as may be appropriate. The patent is kept in force by annual renewal fees, increased from time to time to keep pace with inflation, for a total period of 20 years from application (unless, see p. 14, dated before mid-1967). The inventor has also to pay the fees for filing, search, examination and grant already mentioned. There will also be the modest charges made by the patent agent who drafts the specifications and negotiates with the Patent Office. Foreign patenting will add very greatly to the cost.

Money can of course be saved by not paying renewal fees and letting the patent lapse, but patents that are not kept up for their full term are seldom much use: since all a patent can do is to stop other people using the invention it will not be of value until the invention has reached the stage where other people want to use it. Few inventions are profitable quickly enough to tempt others to infringement in their first years; indeed, inventions of any importance seem seldom to be very profitable until quite late in the life of any patent covering them. Of course, it is often impossible to tell at the beginning what an invention is likely to be worth and, in doubtful cases, it will be better to take out a patent just in case; even so, the published figures suggest that many useless applications are filed.

GRANT AND OWNERSHIP

Inventors in these days are usually employees of some company, and as a rule the company either is entitled to the patent under their service agreements or buys them out before or soon after the application is filed. Arrangements can be made for the patent to be granted to whoever actually owns it—usually a company—even where the application is made by the actual inventor. Once a patent has been sealed it can be bought and sold much like other property, provided the disposition is made in writing and the transaction is registered at the Patent Office. The name of the owner can in theory be found from the register; the names of the applicants appear on the printed copies of the specification sold by the Patent Office and kept on the office files.

A sale or other disposition of the patent may be effective in law if made by those whose names appear on the register of proprietors, whether or not it " really " belongs wholly or in part to someone else. If, therefore, the inventors (for example), or the promoters of a company which is to exploit the invention, wish to retain some control over a patent, it may be wise for them to be registered as part proprietors.

PATENT AGENTS

In practice, the work of negotiating with the Patent Office is done by patent agents, whose profession it is. They also draw up nearly all specifications and are concerned in nearly all Patent Office proceedings and so on. It is theoretically possible for an inventor to do everything himself without professional help, but if a patent is worth applying for at all, the difference made by practised drafting of the specifications and skilled negotiation with the examiner will be worth far more than a patent agent's fees.

NOTE: THE GROUNDS ON WHICH A PATENT MAY BE DECLARED INVALID

The grounds on which patents may be held invalid (by the courts or by the Patent Office) are different for new and for old patents. These grounds are of great practical importance. It should always be borne in mind that while it is usually fairly easy to decide whether a patent is infringed or not (at least, fairly easy to anyone who can read a patent claim in the sort of way lawyers do) it is very seldom easy to decide whether a patent is valid.

Imitating the Product

Thus whenever there is a question of enforcing a patent by court proceedings, the question of validity is likely to be the most important one in the case. It will be seen that while some of the grounds set out below affect the patent as a whole (insufficiency of instructions, for instance) others affect only the claims as such. Where this is so, it is possible for some of the claims to be valid although others are invalid. Such a position gives rise to difficult procedural problems, but for most purposes the important question then is: is any claim that has been (or will be) infringed a valid claim? The other claims matter much less.

Grounds affecting both new and old patents

These are the grounds:

1. *Lack of novelty*: That a claim of the specification includes something which had been published in this country (or used here, either publicly or secretly, but not purely by way of experiment) before the priority date of that claim. The claim is then said to be " anticipated " by the prior publication or prior user (the " prior art ").

It is quite common to find that the first few claims of a specification are broad enough to be invalid on this ground, while the later, narrower claims are not.

2. *Obviousness*: That a claim includes something that was obvious, at its priority date, in view of what had already been published or publicly used in this country before.

This ground also is closely connected with width of claim, so tends to affect only the " main " claims of a patent.

3. *Insufficiency*: That the Complete Specification does not give clear and full enough instructions to enable a skilled man to carry the invention into effect.

It is possible for there to be insufficient instructions to carry some claims into effect, but sufficient for others; but, generally speaking, a specification tends to be sufficient for all claims or insufficient for all.

4. *Obtaining*: That the patent was granted to someone not entitled to it.

This objection takes a rather different form with old patents (that the applicant for the patent was not qualified to apply, or that it was obtained in contravention of the rights of whoever alleges the invalidity); but the effect is much the same.

5. *Not an invention*: That the alleged invention is not the sort of thing that can be patented at all.

Grounds affecting " new " patents only:

Wrongful amendment: That the specification has been altered, so as to disclose something not disclosed in the specification when it was first filed, or has been altered since the patent was granted to make the claims cover something they did not cover before.

Grounds affecting " old " patents only:

1. *Prior claiming*: That the invention (so far as claimed in some claim of the Complete Specification) is already the subject of a valid claim of earlier priority date in another patent.

2. *Ambiguity*: That it is uncertain what a claim means.

3. *Illegality*: " That the primary or intended use or exercise of the invention is contrary to law." (A patent for an improved way of forging bank notes, for instance.)

4. *Inutility*: That the invention (or some forms of it) will not work.

5. *Lack of basis for claims*: That the claims are wider than is justified by what the specification discloses.

6. *Non-disclosure of patentee's best method*: of working the invention, that is.

7. *False suggestion*: That the patentee got his patent by making a false statement.

Note: The Old Application Procedure

Under the old system, a patent application could be accompanied either by a proper specification (" complete specification ") as under the new system, or by a " provisional specification " which served only to give priority (like the earlier applications of the new system). Priority could be obtained by filing an application abroad. and applying here (with a complete specification) as under the new system. If a provisional specification was filed in the first place, the complete had to be filed within 15 months. (The life of the patent runs from the filing of the complete specification.)

This old system continues for any application on which the complete specification has been filed before mid-1978; and such applications result in " old " patents.

Under the old system, search and examination take place without a special request or a further fee; when all objections have been overcome, the patent is not immediately granted, merely " accepted "; the specification is then published. There used then to be provision for others to oppose the grant (on some of the grounds of invalidity); but under the new Act there can be no opposition (even on " old " applications) unless it has been started and " issue joined " before mid-1978.

Note: Inventions by Employees

Not all inventions made by employees belong to their employer: it depends on circumstances. Unless the employee's service agree-

Imitating the Product

ment makes some special arrangement, more favourable to him—an agreement less favourable to the employee is ineffective, except in relation to inventions made before 1978—what governs the matter is whether or not it was the employee's job to make that sort of invention. If so, it belongs to the employer (just as a workman may be employed to make boots, which then belong to the employer, not the workman). If not, it belongs to the employee (even though he may have made it in his employer's time and misappropriated his employer's materials for the purpose). There is no half-way house, except by special agreement; so that if the invention does not belong to the employer, the employee can demand a royalty for its use or even refuse permission to use it. Inventions made before the employment began, or after it stopped, do not belong to the employer.

In deciding what the employee's job was, his general position is naturally crucial. An engineering draughtsman, for instance, is normally expected to improve if he can the design he is drawing out (although a radically new idea may be outside the scope of his employment even though sparked-off by something connected with his work). A factory hand is not normally expected to invent at all. Directors may well be in a position where anything connected with the company's business belongs to the company: by and large, a director must never profit at his company's expense. (The English agent of a foreign engineering concern has been held to be in that sort of position, too.)

Sometimes, there is a special agreement, under which an employee-inventor not merely applies for a patent jointly with his employer (which in itself means nothing) but actually owns his share of the patent. Inventors should note (a) that that sort of agreement is best put into writing, and (b) that the owner of a half-share in a patent cannot (unless the agreement specially says so) do anything with it except himself work the patent—something his employer may be able to do but he will not. (Forming a company to do it is not working the patent: the company will need a licence from both patentees.) Such agreements should be vetted by a solicitor— on both sides.

If the employer does particularly well out of a patented invention made by an employee, the employee can apply (to the Court, or to the Patent Office) to be awarded a fair share of the benefit the employer has got from the invention: unless the rewarding of employees for that sort of invention is already covered by a collective agreement. To qualify for an award, the invention must have been made (not merely patented) after mid-1978; and people who were employed mainly abroad when they made their inventions cannot apply.

NOTE: SOURCES OF THE LAW

For new British patents and European patents covering the United Kingdom, the law is set out in the Patents Act 1977, and the Rules that will be made under it; but this needs to be read in conjunction with the European Patent Convention of 1973 (see s. 130 (7) of the 1977 Act, whatever that subsection may mean). The sections of the Act on international applications need to be read in conjunction with the Patent Co-operation Treaty of 1970 which set up the system. But EEC patents are governed by the Community Patent Convention of 1975, which is itself part of our law. " Old " patents, apart from modification in the Schedules to the 1977 Act, are governed by the Patents Act 1949. The modifications are fairly extensive; but still the basic law is the old law. For this, see the published textbooks: *Blanco White on Patents* (4th ed., 1974) or *Terrell on Patents* (12th ed., 1971).

NOTE: SECURITY RESTRICTIONS

Applicants resident here must apply to patent here (and wait six weeks) before making a patent application abroad, unless our Patent Office permits otherwise. This applies to European, Community and International applications too (they can all be made through our Patent Office), and to most " follow-up " applications as well as the original one for an invention.

4

HOW MUCH USE ARE PATENTS?

The Importance of Validity

Of the patents that are challenged before the courts of law, some are found to be invalid. Since most lawsuits about patents cost at least tens of thousands of pounds, and the larger part of the cost falls on the loser, this is a serious matter for owners of patents. It does not, however, follow that patents are useless; rather this is a measure of success that patents have. It is expensive to challenge the validity of a patent even if the challenge succeeds, and it is hardly ever possible to be sure beforehand that the challenge will succeed. Indeed, at present, though the position may change, it is not common for patents to be held invalid. In the ordinary way, therefore, it is a better proposition commercially to make something outside the " claims " of the patent, than to risk an action for infringement of them. As a rule, it is only the most important patents that are attacked, and even then the attacker will try to find a design that escapes at least the more impressive claims as far as possible. The great majority of patents go through their lives in peace, with nobody really convinced they are valid, but nobody prepared to take the risk of infringing them. Commercially they are just as useful as if they had been valid. Thus, even an invalid patent is often valuable enough to make it worth while keeping on bluffing until the bitter end.

Evading Patents

(a) By " designing round "

A more serious problem is that of the competitor who avoids infringement of a patent. It is much easier to say why a particular patented device is successful and what else would be successful when a product using that device has been on the market for some time, than it was when the specification of the patent was drawn up. The longer a patent lasts the greater the experience at the disposal of competitors. Yet the patent agent who makes out the specification must foresee what in 10 or 20 years' time other manufacturers are likely to want to do, and must frame

How Much Use are Patents?

his "claims" so as to include all these future activities—while at the same time excluding anything that has been published before. In practice, what he does is to guess which features of the new product are going to be important to its success, and make his claims cover whatever combinations of those features are not found in the earlier specifications found by the examiner at the Patent Office. If he guesses right, the patent should be valid and fairly hard to "design round." If he guesses wrong, it will be found later on either that he has "claimed" something only trivially different from the subject of an earlier patent (in which case the new patent will be invalid for obviousness), or that he has confined the monopoly to things having some feature that is not essential—in which case competitors will be able to avoid infringing the patent by omitting that particular feature. (In some countries the courts disregard features shown not to be practically significant; but not in Britain.) Patent agents would be able to guess right more often, if their clients supplied them with more and better information to base their guesses on. As it is, most patents are proof against casual imitators, but not all are proof against a determined attack by competent designers backed by proper legal advice.

Just at present, there is a fair chance that a sympathetic judge will find that the patent is infringed, whatever the "claims" say; but that doesn't solve the problem and leaves everyone uncertain as to what they can do and what they cannot.

(b) By making something "old"

A list of the earlier specifications considered important by the Patent Office examiner in any particular case can be obtained from the Office and one way of avoiding a patent is to go back to one of these earlier inventions. The owner of the later patent is then in a dilemma: if the rival product is within the "claims" of his specification, then his invention is not sufficiently different from the earlier one and his patent must be invalid. This method was apparently used by several American manufacturers when electric shavers first became popular. The Schick shaver, the first to sell in large numbers, was protected by a patent which an American court held valid. Shortly afterwards, several makes of shaver came on to the market closely resembling designs proposed by earlier patents. If the owner of the later patent has made a real technical advance and

Imitating the Product

his specification is skilfully drawn, his product should have a sufficient commercial advantage over earlier designs. If, however, as so often happens, he is only the first to interest the public in an idea and not the first to make it technically successful, then competition based on earlier designs may be very damaging. No system of patents can enable him to stop competition of this sort: he must rely on such commercial advantages as the goodwill he has built up, helped perhaps by enough patents and registered designs to make it impossible for rival products to look the same as his.

As ways of avoiding patents go, this method of digging up an old design is reasonably safe. But it is never completely safe. If what is now made is exactly what was made (or described) before the patent, then certainly any claim that covers it must be invalid. Nearly always, though, some alteration in the old design will be needed, if only to make it suitable for production. Then a quite different question arises, whether the changes to the old design were obvious changes to make before the date of the patent. The answer may easily be, that they became obvious changes to make only when the owner of the patent had shown that there was a market for something close to the old design. But if that is so, it is possible for the patent to be both valid and infringed. In the *Schick* case, for instance, the infringer who was successfully sued in America had based his designs on that of a patent much older than Schick's—but he had altered it just too much.

Most firms will prefer not to take this risk unless the matter is of real commercial importance, so that in the ordinary way the patent will be almost as useful to its owner as if the earlier design had never been published. As we saw in Chapter 2, the value of a patent depends greatly on its not being too important.

LICENSING

The general principle

So far we have only considered patent monopolies as a means of keeping imitations off the market. There is another way of exploiting a patent: the grant of licences. If the patent is valid, the manufacture, importation, sale or use of a patented article (or of articles made by a patented process or machine) are each only lawful if the patentee gives permission for them. Such permission is what is known as a "licence." Subject to the exceptions mentioned below, a patentee can charge what he likes for the licence and make what rules he likes for its exercise. For those who do not wish to manufacture under the patent themselves, and for many who do manufacture themselves, this is the normal way of making money out of a patent.

Permission to use and sell is implied where the patentee made the product himself or licensed its making, but even so the permission may be given subject to express limitations or conditions. Anyone who buys the article knowing of these conditions must either comply with them or risk being sued for infringement of the patent. Not every sort of limitation or condition, though, is allowed.

The main restriction here arises from the EEC rules about "exhaustion of rights": once a patented article has been put on the market in the EEC, by the owner of the patent or with his licence, only in very special circumstances—nobody knows what these might be—can anything afterwards done with that article infringe the patent. This means, in particular, that although it may be allowable to restrict a licensee to manufacturing under the patent only in one EEC country, the patent cannot be used to stop the things he makes being sold throughout the EEC. Even a licence to manufacture in a single country only would probably fall foul of the broader EEC rules forbidding agreements that distort competition within the Common Market. Indeed, the EEC Commission has shown itself hostile to exclusive licences of all sorts; as well as to any terms in licence agreements that try to give the owner of the patent more than his patent itself does.

Our own law also contains some specific restrictions on the terms there can be in licence agreements: in particular, the licensee cannot normally be compelled to buy unpatented materials from the licensor (though he may be given preferential terms if he does, so long as the EEC rules mentioned above are not transgressed); and the licensee cannot be stopped from putting an end to the licence once the original patents have expired (though he can, subject again to EEC rules, be required by the licence to stop manufacturing if he does).

5
PATENTING IMPORTANT INVENTIONS

INTRODUCTION

EVERY now and then, somebody makes a really important invention. As a rule nobody knows this has happened until too late, and it is found either that the man who made the crucial step did not bother to apply for a patent at all, or that his application was considered just as a matter of routine, so that he got the sort of patent we discussed in the last chapter: a patent that would do very well to cover some minor improvement, but will stand neither a determined challenge to its validity nor a determined attempt to escape from its "claims." In that case, the invention can be used by any one prepared to spend a little time and money upon research and rather more upon litigation. Sometimes, though, the inventor—or the inventor's employer—knows he is on to a good thing. What should he do about it?

WHERE OTHERS HAVE TRIED

If the invention is one that a lot of people have been trying to make there may well be very little to be done about it, except get whatever patent the Patent Office will grant and hope for the sympathy of the court in due course. For in that case the files of the Patent Office will contain dozens or hundreds of specifications dealing with the subject, and some of them will almost certainly have come too close to the right answer for there to be much left to patent. In theory, of course, the failure of many other workers to make the invention is strong evidence that it was a good and patentable invention, rather than something obvious; but in practice, the drafting of valid claims that are broad enough to give real protection for the invention is impossible where there have been too many earlier proposals. Some big firms especially make a point of patenting every slight advance in research into such subjects; partly in the hope that if one of their competitors finds the answer they will have patents of their own important enough to bargain with, partly for the very purpose of making it difficult or impossible for competitors to get valid patents. The independent inventor, hoping to make a large fortune by research in competition with the research departments of such large firms, is for this reason almost certainly wasting his time, however brilliant the work he is doing. He would probably make more money by research in some field that is specialised enough for his success not to be a serious challenge to his bigger rivals.

An Important Invention

Let us consider then the case of a manufacturer who is in possession of an invention that he believes is important, and that is unexpected enough to offer a chance of a really valuable patent. It will have to be a valid patent, for it is sure to come under hostile scrutiny as soon as its importance is understood; and it must have " claims " that are wide in scope, so that competitors cannot escape from it except by spending large sums upon research. It follows that attention will have to be paid to legal technicalities, which means extra trouble and extra expense in applying for the patent—though they will be trifling compared with the trouble of fighting a lawsuit later on, and the expense that will be incurred even if the suit is successful.

(a) The initial application

The first step will be the filing of an application accompanied by an informal specification. It will be worth giving more care than usual to the drafting of this, so as to be certain that it both includes as much detailed information as possible and foreshadows the claims that will be incorporated in the final specification. In this connection, it must not be forgotten that those claims will have to be broad ones: they must cover not only the actual machine or process that the inventor would like to see used commercially but also any alternative form of the invention that competitors may want to use—or that competitors may be prepared to use if compelled to do so by the need to avoid the patent. In order to be sure that such broad claims will hold as " priority date " the date of the original application, some basis for them must be laid in the original specification: both by indicating the general principles of operation of the invention, and by suggesting alternatives to whatever is actually described in detail in the specification. Many inventors dislike including descriptions of alternatives that they believe to be inferior, but it ought to be done. If the alternatives later turn out to be hopelessly inferior, they can be abandoned when the final specification is drawn up.

Imitating the Product

It may be desirable to file more than one preliminary application, so as to get the best priority for further discoveries made from time to time. As was explained in Chapter 3, though, the definitive application should not be left too long, in case competitors try to patent something similar.

(b) Protection abroad

It will soon be necessary to consider patenting abroad: even a company not able to contemplate manufacturing abroad or bringing infringement actions abroad to protect an export market, may want to license foreign manufacturers and get something back that way. (Even a foreign manufacturer who is really interested mainly in " knowhow " will often be unwilling to sign a satisfactory agreement, unless there are patents in his home country to hang the agreement on.)

First, Europe. The initial application can be filed here: a British application can found priority in Europe as well as a European one can. But before any application is filed that is meant to be proceeded with, a decision will have to be taken whether in Europe to seek separate national patents, or a European or an EEC patent: or one of these and a British patent too. (See Chap. 3; and note that if both British and EEC or European patents are wanted, either a single international application must be made for them—see below—or both applications must be filed on the same day; otherwise one will anticipate the other.)

In countries outside the European system, the initial British application (or applications) can again be used to give priority. Almost all industrial countries are parties to an international convention concerning patent rights, which allows residents of any such country to file a patent application at home, and then within a specified period (normally 12 months) to file corresponding applications in the rest of such countries " as of " the date of his home application. Most countries place applications under the convention at some disadvantage. It might therefore seem desirable to make entirely separate applications at home and in certain foreign countries. But the European system of informal applications is exceptional, so such foreign applications would normally have to wait until a specification corresponding to our final specification could be prepared. This would involve a loss in priority. Further, some countries refuse altogether to patent otherwise than under the convention an invention that is already patented elsewhere. The normal practice is

Patenting Important Inventions

consequently to make foreign applications by means of the convention, accepting the disadvantages that result and ignoring the smaller countries which are not parties to it.

It is going to be possible to avoid the trouble and expense of preparing and filing separate applications for all the countries where patents are wanted, by filing an "international application." Such an application will be made (so far as United Kingdom residents are concerned) to our own Patent Office, which will hand it over to a foreign office specialising in the subject-matter concerned. There they will search against it, and publish it (18 months from application); also, if the applicant wants, they will reach preliminary conclusions on novelty and obviousness (which some countries' Patent Offices will no doubt adopt). The application will then be passed to the Patent Offices of those countries working this system in which the applicant wants patents; probably all the major industrial countries will belong, and so will the European Patent Office (so that an international application will be able to seek an EEC or European patent, as well as patents outside Europe and in individual European countries). The system should be cheaper and much less trouble than applying separately everywhere. On the other hand, different countries' patent systems tend to call for different sorts of patent specification, and it may if the case is important enough pay to have a separate specification drafted for some countries. Furthermore, if there is an international preliminary examination for obviousness, it is likely to be stricter than some countries —such as this one—would carry out, so that separate applications in such countries might stand a better chance of success. For most purposes, though, it looks as if the making of international applications will usually be desirable, where more than a very few foreign patents are wanted.

(c) The specification

Next will come the preparation of the final specification. It must be filed within 12 months of the first application in any case, and unless foreign patenting is to be handled entirely by an international application will have to be ready long enough before then for specifications based on it to be filed at Patent Offices abroad within the 12-month period. Before the filing, two things should be done, though both are often omitted. First, the inventor should set to work to discover the secret of his own success and, when he has, should put the answer into a further specification.

Imitating the Product

Second, a draft of the specification should be shown to counsel: this necessarily adds to the cost, and in simple cases, or cases not of the greatest importance, it should be sufficient to take the advice of counsel later on—when the Patent Office examiner's comments on the specification are received.

It was explained in the previous chapter that for a patent to be fully effective, the distinguishing features of the " invention " (as listed in the claims of the specification) must all be features that play a real part in the success of the new device. The system of guessing which features matter is too risky when the patent will be important: so the specification must be drawn up by someone who knows what the vital points are.

Where counsel comes in

The points that make specifications so difficult to draw up are lawyers' points. They depend on the words of the specification—that is, they depend on the meaning that a court of law will give to those words, for lawyers treat words rather differently from most other people. If the patent is ever the subject of an action at law, much of the argument in court will be about words. Now a patent agent is not primarily concerned with legal matters. He drafts many specifications, but he seldom has an opportunity to hear one of them analysed in a court of law. Most of his work lies between his clients and the staff of the Patent Office, and in either case he will be dealing with people whose experience is technical rather than legal. Further, the points which cause the most difficulty in court proceedings are precisely those over which the staff of the Patent Office do not normally trouble themselves, so that a patent agent will seldom be required to consider them, and may have few opportunities of gaining experience in handling them. The result is that, however good a job the patent agent makes of the specification, the final responsibility for its wording ought in a case of sufficient importance to be placed upon counsel.

(d) The Patent Office examination

The applicant will not at this stage yet know whether his patent is going to be a satisfactory one. He will not know this until his invention has been compared with those in earlier specifications, and it usually pays in practice to leave the job of searching for these earlier documents to the examiners at the Patent Offices concerned. Nor can the claims of the specification receive their final form until the examiner's comments have been received. If the specification has been well drawn up the examiner may not have any serious objection to make: he will almost certainly find something to comment upon in the wording of the specification. It does sometimes happen that his search produces nothing. This is inconvenient since it leaves the patent agent handling the case in the dark as to what earlier documents there are. To avoid this, the draftsman will sometimes "draw a search" by including initially a broader claim than he considers himself entitled to. Further, it may be advisable to make even the most half-hearted objection by an examiner an excuse for quite large alterations in the "claims"; for the claims are being framed less with a view to satisfying the examiner than with a view to what a judge may say later on. It may prove desirable in this country to frame the specification in a way to which the examiner will object; examiners are not trained lawyers, and have a lot of work to get through, and naturally tend to prefer standard patent jargon and standard forms of claim to anything new. This is fine for doubtful inventions, since the incomprehensibility of the jargon makes it harder for the patentee's competitors to decide whether the claims mean anything or not, are anticipated or not. A court, less conditioned to the jargon, may take a different view of it. Besides, sooner or later new sorts of claim become desirable: claims for ways of operating an electric computer, and such like. There has to be a first of such things, and any good examiner will probably notice and question it.

If necessary, disagreements with the examiner must be disposed of by obtaining a "hearing," that is, by going to the Patent Office and arguing the point with one of the higher officials. If he in turn is not persuaded it will be necessary to appeal to the Patents Court.

(e) Amendment

The examiner's search usually uncovers a representative collection of the published documents on which later attacks on a patent might be based, while the applicants themselves will usually know what sort of thing was made and used in this country up to the date of the application. Sometimes, however, a publication will turn up later on which was not considered when the specification was drafted, and which seriously threatens the validity of the patent. This is particularly likely to happen where foreign documents are

Imitating the Product

concerned and in industries that are not very well developed in this country. Or it may turn out that something too close to the claims of the patent was publicly used, either in this country or abroad, before the date of the application, the applicants not knowing of it (or omitting to mention it to their patent agent). The validity of the patent can then only be secured by "amending" the specification: that is, by altering the claims so as to narrow them down until they no longer include whatever it is that has turned out to have been unpatentable. Amendment can be left until the last minute, when court proceedings about the patent have started or are contemplated, but it is nearly always far better to amend as soon as the patent is found to be invalid; amendment is easier then (for it is less likely to be opposed) and fewer problems will arise afterwards. In particular, the patentee ought not to leave in his specification claims he knows to be invalid, and if he does so, when in due course he does apply for amendment, he may be required to explain the reasons for delay. This occurred in *Raleigh* v. *Miller* (1950) (where the explanation was not accepted) and *Weiss's Patent* (1949) (where it was). In the case of a patent whose specification was drafted without especially full investigation of the invention and its potentialities for future developments, the specification is likely to be defective anyway by reason of matters not known to the draftsman, so that amendment is worth considering as soon as the patent is found to be important enough to be worth spending money on.

Amendment of the specification requires the permission of the Patent Office or, if the patent is the subject of an action pending in the court at the time, of the court. Permission to amend is not very difficult to obtain but is subject to the limitations: that it is not possible to widen the " claims " (so that nothing can infringe after amendment unless it infringed before); and that it is not possible to add completely new matter (so that it is not possible, for instance, to cure by amendment a failure to give adequate instructions to carry out the invention, nor to add a new feature which was not mentioned in the specification and has since been found essential to the working of the invention). Further, amendment of the specification may make it impossible to recover damages for infringements that took place before amendment. The result is that while the power to amend is a very useful weapon, it is a poor substitute for successful drafting of a specification in the first place.

THE ACTION FOR INFRINGEMENT

The first action in which a patent is involved is vital for that patent—such an action is usually fought once and for all. If the patentee loses, it means either that his patent is found invalid and the grant is revoked or that the claims of the specification are declared to be too narrow to cover the articles the defendant is making. In the former case there is no longer any patent, in the latter everyone in the industry now knows how to get round it. If he wins, on the other hand, his competitors will probably respect that patent in future: there are always other things to make and sell that do not involve a patent action. Furthermore, if the patent is held valid, the patentee will receive a " certificate of contested validity," which, while not forbidding others to challenge the validity of the patent or to claim they are not infringing it, will make it very expensive for them to do so. (The actual effect of a certificate is to entitle the patentee, if he wins another action on that patent, to ask for " solicitor and own client costs " instead of " party and party costs " for the action. " Party and party costs " are supposed to correspond to the least amount it would be possible to spend in fighting the action, " solicitor and own client costs " to what has actually been spent. The difference, for a patent action, may be very large.)

Delayed actions

It was emphasised in Chapter 1 that, in most cases, if a patent action is going to be fought at all, the sooner it is started the better. Equally, there are cases where an action should not be started at all. For example, a patent of dubious validity may be of considerable commercial value, being respected by most competitors. If someone does pluck up enough courage to infringe it, it may be better to buy him off, with a licence at low rates (or even free of royalty) rather than risk suing. It may be better thus to buy off a whole series of competitors—a sort of game of sardines. If, on the other hand, the patent is probably valid, and infringers are not of great importance compared with those who respect the patent or pay royalties, it may be worth while waiting until the patent has almost expired and then cleaning up by demanding damages from infringers—rather than upsetting things by suing earlier. (In any case, where an infringer is not sued right away, consideration should be given to notifying him of the existence of the patent, to stop him pleading innocence later.) Again: suppose a com-

Imitating the Product

petitor finds a way round the patent, and tries to patent his alternative. The immediate reaction of most businessmen is to attack his patent. It is the wrong reaction. The right thing to do is to encourage him to have his patent, to stop other rats using the same hole.

From the point of view of an intending imitator of the patented article, there is a serious risk that he may be allowed to make his imitation for several years and may then be faced with a claim for a very large sum in damages. He can bring an action before he starts manufacturing, asking the court to declare that the article he proposes to manufacture will not infringe the patent concerned. He may also ask the court to revoke the patent on the ground that it is invalid. The proceedings in either case are nearly as expensive as ordinary actions for infringement, and may be rather easier for the patentee to win.

Threats

A threat of proceedings for infringement of patent can be very worrying to the recipient. Naturally, a manufacturer who infringes, or the importer of an infringing article made abroad, should expect the patentee to say " If you do not stop I shall sue you." But threats to a man's customers are another matter: they are unlikely to want to get involved, and will usually quietly stop buying his goods rather than face an action. So it is provided that anyone aggrieved by threats of an infringement action can sue for damages and for an injunction preventing further threats, " unless the defendant . . . proves that the acts in respect of which proceedings were threatened constitute or, if done, would constitute an infringement of a patent "—and the patent is not shown to be invalid. But there is this exception, that if the only threat is to sue for making or importing something (or for using a patented process) no action lies. (Taken literally, this exception does not cover a threat to sue the manufacturer or importer for selling the goods concerned; but the courts will probably say that Parliament cannot have meant to be as silly as that.)

Since it is very seldom possible to be certain of proving that any particular act is an infringement of a patent, or to be sure that any claim in a patent specification will not be found invalid, this provision is a dangerous trap for unwary owners of patents.

Misuse of Patents

The owner of a patent ought to make use of his invention if he can; certainly he ought not to use his patent for preventing all use of his invention. In the hope of preventing such misuse of patents, provisions of one sort or another have for many years been inserted in the Patents Acts; in particular there have been provisions by which anyone who wants to use an invention and can show that the patents covering it are being misused in certain ways can apply to the Patent Office for a compulsory licence, enabling him to use those patents upon payment of a proper royalty. The application cannot be made for three years after the patent has been granted. Compulsory licence provisions have never proved effective, and the present ones are hardly ever used.

Patents are not in practice used for suppressing new ideas; the difficulty with anything really new is to get anyone to take it up. The few applications for compulsory licences that are made are not concerned with inventions that have been suppressed, but with inventions that have already proved profitable—where the patentee wants to keep the profit to himself.

" Improvement " Patents

If a patent proves really profitable, its owner will want to go on profiting from the invention after his patent expires. There is a way in which a monopoly in an important invention may be kept alive after the patent has come to an end, and that is by patenting large numbers of minor improvements to the original invention. Provided the patented improvements represent genuine development over the period during which the original patent is in force, and provided they are patented with determination and persistence, by the time the original patent expires a would-be imitator should be faced with this situation: that the article described in the original specification is too inferior to contemporary designs to be commercially saleable, while he cannot equal the newer models without risking an action for infringement of so many of the improvement patents, that he would almost certainly lose in respect of some patent or other. Even if he were to win the action on enough of the patents to let him go on manufacturing without any fundamental change in his design, the cost of fighting and losing the action as a whole would still take much of the profit

Imitating the Product

out of his venture. For this reason the existence of a mass of improvement patents is often a sufficient deterrent to would-be imitators. The original manufacturer's position need not deteriorate with further lapse of time: he should always be some years ahead in design so far as patentable improvements are concerned, while the longer he keeps the field to himself the greater the advantage he has in manufacturing experience. His monopoly will last until some competitor comes along with the skill needed to "design round" the more dangerous patents and the courage to fight a patent action if necessary; how long this will be will depend as usual on the importance of the market covered by the monopoly, as well as on the rate at which he continues to devise new patentable improvements. In the past, such monopolies have sometimes lasted a long time.

Where the owner of the original patent is himself the manufacturer, the patenting of improvements presents no particular difficulty. Where, however, the main patent is exploited by licensing someone else to manufacture in return for payment of a royalty on production, the patentee will find it difficult not to lose control as soon as the original patent expires. For the developments on which improvement patents can be based will be made by the manufacturer, who will also have the practical experience; the new patents will naturally belong to him and the monopoly given by them will belong to him, too. Sometimes the manufacturer can be persuaded to agree that the original patentee shall become the owner of the improvement patents, but such arrangements are probably illegal under EEC law.

It is in general very difficult for an inventor who is not actively engaged in an industry to keep any substantial control over it by means of patents. Cases do still occur from time to time of inventors making large fortunes by using their inventions to build up large manufacturing businesses, while other inventors do well enough by selling their patents to existing firms and at the same time getting important posts with those firms as consultants or designers. The inventor who makes any large sum simply by the sale or licensing of his patents seems to be very rare.

TAXATION AND PATENTS

Patents are subject to special rules as to income tax. Royalties are not allowable as business expenses of the manufacturer who pays them (so that they have to be paid out of taxed profits, if he has any profits to tax); instead, whoever pays the royalty out of taxed income should deduct tax before paying and may then keep it. (If he had no profits (*i.e.* no taxed income) to pay the royalties out of he must deduct the tax and hand it over to the Revenue.) Furthermore, capital sums paid for patents and patent licences (but not sums paid for know-how) are treated as income of the seller spread over a six-year period; this being balanced by allowing the purchaser annual allowances on what he has paid. (This is not quite as hard on inventors as it seems: for a professional inventor must reckon the proceeds of sale of patents as income anyway. It is hard on purely amateur inventors, but they have too few votes to matter.) The position of foreign patentees needs watching here: they naturally tend to demand that a British licensee agree to pay royalties (and even more, capital sums) free of tax. There are, in fact, agreements in force with most foreign countries under which a foreigner can get payment in full (in the case of royalties, the payer is compensated for the tax he would otherwise have deducted and kept); but the foreign patentee has to make the request, and licence agreements ought to be specially framed accordingly.

NOTE: PATENTING DRUGS AND SIMILAR CHEMICAL COMPOUNDS

(*a*) *Problems*

The effective patenting of newly invented drugs and the like presents special difficulties. The fundamental problem is this. If the drug concerned is an entirely new chemical, its discoverer will be entitled to patent it; but just because it is entirely new, he will be unable to tell what related substances will be so similar in their effects as to be just as good. If he attempts to guess what other substances will work, he may well guess hopelessly wrong; if he confines himself to those he really knows about, his competitors (who have been told by his success what sort of thing to look for) will be able to market some related substance not covered by him. The preparation and trial of any new drug is a long job, and even the biggest research laboratories can try out only a few likely compounds at a time. To a certain extent the difficulty can be overcome by the power of amendment, but this is seldom a completely satisfactory answer. The inventor's main safeguard is the cost of testing and marketing a related substance; but if the drug is profitable enough, that may be worth doing.

Even worse difficulties face the man who discovers how to prepare a substance that already exists in nature (a vitamin, for instance, or something like penicillin); for there are bound to be other ways of doing the job that he cannot cover. Further, the man who discovers a new and valuable property of an old sub-

Imitating the Product

stance (the insecticidal properties of D.D.T., for example) must be very clever to get any sort of patent at all, even to cover the stuff as sold. He should be able to get a patent to cover a process of using the stuff in agriculture (not, though, use in medicine); but collection of royalties or finding out about infringements may be very difficult. To deal with discoveries of new medical or veterinary uses of known compounds, the Act has a new sort of patent: a patent for the compound " for " the newly discovered use. The intention is that the owner of the patent will then be able to sue anyone who sells the stuff, knowing or intending it to be used for the new treatment.

It might be thought that such inventions were particularly valuable and needed to be specially encouraged; but the law is more concerned with restricting such patents than with encouraging them.

(b) " Selection " patents

There is a special sort of invention that turns up fairly often in the field of chemistry, and leads to what are called " selection patents." When a new and valuable chemical compound is discovered—a new drug, perhaps, or a new sort of dyestuff—it will usually at once be apparent to a skilled chemist that innumerable other, closely related compounds may be as good or better. But there is usually still room for invention in making those compounds, one by one, and finding out which really are as good or better; and even more room for invention in seeing without making them all which others will be as good or better. This picking-out of the useful ones, from a large class which is already known in general terms, is known as " selection." The courts have laid down certain rules governing patents for such inventions: in particular, the specification must explain in what way the selected ones are better than the rest: and they must really be better, and better than almost all of the others. And, of course, this must be something that only an inventor could have foreseen. These rules probably still apply.

NOTE: THE DEFINITION OF INFRINGEMENT

We have a new definition of infringement, applying to old as well as to new patents. Something very similar applies to EEC patents. Most of the activities that amount to infringement are what one might expect: making, selling, importing, using a patented article; working a patented process or selling, importing or using the product. But it is also an infringement to " keep " the article or product; or knowingly to supply the means for working an invention, unless what is supplied is a " staple commercial product "—and even then it is infringement if the supply is intended to induce the recipient to infringe.

On the other hand, there are general exceptions: for things done privately and not commercially (it is not at all clear what " privately " means here: probably, " privately as distinct from

Patenting Important Inventions

commercially "); for experiments with the invention; for the making-up of individual medical prescriptions; for use by foreign ships and aircraft. There is also a special provision protecting those who used or prepared to use the invention before the priority date of the patent: they may go on doing what they did or prepared to do before. (This last provision is necessary, because use of an invention only invalidates a subsequent patent for it if the use makes the invention public, and manufacturing processes may well not be made public.)

Note: The " Old " Law

This chapter has mostly set out the " new " law; there are differences for " old " patents.

Patents of addition: Some " old " patents are " patents of addition " (it says so, at the head of printed specification). They are for " improvements or modifications " of the invention of an earlier patent. They expire when the earlier (" main ") patent expires; but do not need to show invention (as distinct from novelty) over the " main " invention. They do not carry renewal fees.

Actions for declarations or non-infringement; Actions for threats; Certificates of contested validity: On these subjects, the old rules were not the same as the new ones; and it is very difficult to say which rules will apply to patents " dated " before mid-1978 (*i.e.* patents granted under the old procedure). So: it may be that, in an action for a declaration that an " old " patent is not infringed, the plaintiff pays the costs, win or lose. It may be that a threat to sue for infringement of an " old " patent is unlawful, even if made against a manufacturer or importer. It may be that a certificate of validity for an " old " patent, unless given after an action for infringement committed after mid-1978, does not put its owner in as good a position as we have said.

Extension of patents: The old law made provision for extending the lives of patents whose owners had made too little out of them, considering how the invention benefited the public; and a few extended patents do exist. For the future, extension is limited to patents which have only a 16-year life (*i.e.* of which the complete specification was filed before mid-1967): such patents can have their life extended to 20 years but no further.

Definition of infringement: Although the new definition applies to " old " patents, things done before 1978 are judged by the old law. Furthermore, an act begun before 1978, which was not then an infringement, can be continued after 1978 without becoming an infringement. This exception, like the exception for things done before the patent (see the previous Note) is very narrow: any significant alteration in what was previously done could take the case out of the exception. This means that a previously used process probably cannot be modernised; even enlarging the old plant could be held to involve infringement.

6

INDUSTRIAL DESIGNS

INTRODUCTION

FOR many years now, our law has included protection for industrial designs: that is for the artistic element in manufactured products. Until 1968 the basis of that protection was registration, and it was thought that manufactured products which had no artistic element (*e.g.* spare parts for machinery) were not protected at all, except in those rare instances where there was a separate patent. The position has radically changed since the Design Copyright Act of 1968. This Act in its express terms only dealt with artistic designs, but it made people think about ordinary copyright in the industrial field and it was not very long before they saw that ordinary copyright gave protection to non-artistic designs as well as artistic designs.

Now, the owner of an industrial design may enforce any copyrights he has against those who copy his design, but only during a period of 15 years from the date when articles bearing the design are first marketed by him; after that, use of the design ceases to be an infringement of copyright. In relation to a design which has no artistic element—no eye appeal to the customer—it seems that the owner may enforce any copyrights he may own for a period of 50 years from the year of the death of the author, although there is still some room for argument as to whether the period is just the same as for artistic designs. This latter provision has evoked considerable criticism and the Committee considering the law of Copyright (the Whitford Committee) could not make up its mind as to precisely what the law should be. However in any new Copyright Act it is likely that the present position will be changed at least to reduce the period of protection and, possibly also, the degree of protection in that injunctions would no longer be obtainable.

CONSEQUENCES OF 1968 ACT

The 1968 Act has had far-reaching consequences. Registration of industrial designs was never very common; in recent years, there have been about 4,500 registrations a year and about three-quarters of all registrations are dropped after five years. It seems likely that this number, which has fallen by a quarter since 1968, will dwindle further, and it has been proposed that registered design protection should be repealed. But copyright requires no registration beforehand, so that the owner of a design that is copied will quite often find that he is in a position to stop the copying by an action for infringement of copyright—and to stop it promptly, if he acts promptly, by securing an interlocutory injuncetion in his action. (Compare in Chap. 1, the remarks on interlocutory injunctions in patent actions.) What is more, very rarely indeed can a manufacturer who wants to copy now feel confident that copying will not leave him open to an action for infringement of copyright. This was a major change: in the past the basic rule was that it was lawful to copy another's product, in the absence of special circumstances. Now the rule is that unless it is certain that the thing to be copied has been on the market for over 15 years, copying a product is not safe unless major changes are made in its appearance. Even if it has been on the market for over 15 years, it will still not be safe if it is a design which has no eye appeal.

The Present Law

Since the 1968 Act, the requirements for an action for infringement of copyright by making and selling a manufactured article may be summarised as follows. First, there must be a copyright artistic work: either the original model of the article itself (if it is such as will qualify as a copyright work—see below) or drawings for it. Secondly, there must be an infringing article: an article which (without the copyright owner's consent) has been copied, directly or indirectly, from the copyright work—"reproduces" the work, in the language of the Copyright Act 1956. Thirdly, you need a defendant for the action: the man who made the copy (if it was made in this country) or someone who has or had possession of it. And, fourthly, in the case of artistic designs, there is the 15-year time limit: if the design is not dictated solely by function, the copy must have been made less than 15 years after the copyright owner first marketed articles embodying the design. The first three of these call for a little more discussion.

The Copyright Work

If the design started life as a set of drawings then, regardless of their artistic merit, these will almost certainly be copyright unless they were made before the present Copyright

Imitating the Product

Act came into force in June 1957. (If they were made before then, and they were meant as drawings of an industrial article, there will normally be no copyright covering the article.) Thus, for instance, in *British Northrop* v. *Texteam Blackburn* (1974), a case concerning spare machine parts, engineering drawings of a rivet, a screw, a bolt and a washer were copyright works, and were not disqualified on grounds of simplicity. However, there is a complication concerning " reproduction " of drawings by three-dimensional articles: see below. So a plaintiff will find it easier to rely on the original three-dimensional article as his " copyright work " if he can. But a three-dimensional industrial article may or may not have copyright (quite apart from the point about pre-1957 designs). If it was a " sculpture " it will have copyright, and that word probably covers most moulded articles. Otherwise, it can be copyright only as a " work of artistic craftsmanship," which calls for hand-work going beyond mere assembly or machining. In the leading case on the subject, *George Hensher* v. *Restawile Upholstery* (1976) the House of Lords gave a number of interpretations of this phrase, none of which is completely satisfactory. It seems clear, however, that the article must merit the epithet " artistic " and that its production must involve craftsmanship. Thus, other things being equal, a striking and complex design is more likely to receive acceptance as an " artistic work " than a simple and commonplace one.

" REPRODUCTION "

In the sort of dispute we are contemplating here, there will seldom be any evidence of copying by the defendant apart from the resemblance between his article and the plaintiff's. The court will then have to consider two related questions: Has there been copying? and: In the final result, does the defendant's article "reproduce" the plaintiff's copyright work (or a substantial part of that work)? Where the plaintiff's "work" is his product itself, these are straightforward questions, although they may not be easy to answer, especially where the defendant's design differs from the plaintiff's. (Again, a plaintiff whose design is striking and complex will find the court easier to convince.) Where the plaintiff's product is a moulded article, and the defendant has simply made moulds from a sample and so reproduced it almost exactly, copying should be immediately obvious; and this is a common sort of copying in these days. The difficult cases are those where the defendant's design is really his own design, influenced by the plaintiff's, and the court has to decide where mere influence ends and copying begins.

Reproduction from drawings

Where on the other hand, the plaintiff has to rely on a drawing as his copyright work, there is a further question to be answered: for there is no infringement in such cases if the defendant's article " would not appear, to persons who are not experts in relation to objects of that description, to be a reproduction of " the drawing (Copyright Act, s. 9 (8)). It is not altogether clear what this means, but there is no reported case of this defence succeeding. In one case a judge held that in view of this provision a boat did not reproduce the " general arrangement " drawing of the plans it was built from—and the Court of Appeal unanimously inclined to the opposite opinion (*Dorling* v. *Honnor* (1964)). It seems that it is for the court to put aside any expertise which it may have in relation to drawings of the type in issue and reach its own conclusion as a non-expert.

Who May Be Sued

This is a subject discussed in more detail in Chapter 19. Briefly: infringement of copyright is committed, once and for all, when an unauthorised reproduction is made of a copyright work, if that is done in this country. But once an article is an infringing copy of a work, or an article is imported into this country whose making would have infringed if it had been done here, then the copyright owner is entitled to treat that copy as belonging to him: to demand that it be given up to him, and to claim damages if it is sold or otherwise disposed of—damages which will be assessed on the basis that the infringing copies actually belonged to the copyright owner. There is some protection against liability for damages for those who had already disposed of the copies when they first learnt of the infringement. The copyright owner is equally entitled to demand moulds, etc., in which infringing copies were made. So that even if the manufacturer or importer can claim exemption from damages through innocence, the copyright owner will normally be entitled to an injunction against his doing it again, and will be able to proceed against the infringing copies in the hands of customers.

Care of Copyrights

Although copyrights come into existence automatically, it is unwise to forget about them entirely. They are of limited value if their owner cannot prove he has them. So the first date of marketing of any new product—which governs the effective life of the copyright, see page 13—ought to be carefully recorded, and all original models and drawings for the product ought to be carefully preserved, with a note of who contributed to them. The service agreements of people who make designs ought to cover the question of copyright ownership. And so on.

Designs that are Registered

Where designs are registered, the question is not one of copying, but merely of resemblance: the court has to consider whether the registered design and the defendant's design are in substance the same or not. But there is also a question of novelty: the registration is invalid unless the design shows substantial novelty over its predecessors. (So an action for infringement of a registered design tends to be half-way between a patent action and a copyright action.) Since the design must be novel when registered, registration must be applied for before the article is marketed, which means incurring fees before it is clear which designs are going to be worth protecting. This has discouraged most companies from making much use of design registrations in the past. But there are some designs that ought to be registered because copyright will not cover them: designs which need never be copied because a rival designer if he thinks hard enough will sooner or later reach the same answer independently. Of course, where two designs are closely similar a court will be sceptical of evidence that they were made independently; but if in fact they were, and the defendant can prove it, then a copyright action must fail (for there will have been no " reproduction " by the defendant) but an action on a registered design may still succeed. However, such cases are rare. (*Cow* v. *Cannon* (1959) could be one of them.) A design registration takes a few months to secure (so may not be available for immediate use against rapid copying). It lasts for five years in the first instance, and may be renewed for two further periods of five years each. Further information may be found in P.I.R.D.

7

CROWN RIGHTS AND SECURITY

THE CROWN'S RIGHT TO WORK PATENTS

ANY government department may use, or authorise others to use, any patented invention "for the services of the Crown." Mostly, this means for the armed forces—although some drugs for British hospitals have been procured under these powers. The proprietor of the patent is entitled to compensation for any use by the Government in this way but he cannot prevent that use. If the invention was one that any government department knew about (otherwise than because its owner told them about it) before the patent was applied for, this does not of itself make the patent invalid but it disentitles the owner to compensation for any Government use.

Surplus patented articles, originally made for Government use, may be freely sold. So may articles confiscated by the Customs or Excise. So may medical supplies. During a war period and for war purposes, or for national purposes during a period of emergency, or in respect of inventions concerned with atomic energy, government departments may authorise anyone to sell such articles whether originally made for Government use or not—subject to the usual rights to compensation. Our Government may also have weapons and munitions made here for our allies, or the United Nations, and sell them to the government or organisation concerned. Except in these cases the Government has no right to authorise the sale of such articles without permission from the proprietor of the patent concerned.

If a firm authorised by the Government to use an invention is already licensed to do so by the proprietor of it, the royalties fixed by the licence need not be paid so far as the Government use is concerned. Such a licensee may still be liable to make some payments to the proprietor: guaranteed minimum royalties, for instance (see *No-Nail Cases* v. *No-Nail Boxes* (1944)). In general, however, the proprietor must rely on his right to demand compensation from the Crown. The amount of compensation, if it cannot be agreed, will normally be settled by referring the whole matter to the High Court. The Crown is supposed to let inventors know that it is using their patents, but it

Imitating the Product

tends not to (especially where military secrets are involved) and the inventor's main problem tends to be to find out what use if any is being made of his invention.

There are similar provisions allowing Crown use of registered designs.

KEEPING INVENTIONS SECRET

It is necessary to prevent the automatic publication of specifications of inventions of military importance. It is therefore provided, first, that such inventions may be communicated to and tried out by any Service department without prejudicing a subsequent patent application; and, secondly, that, if an application is made to patent such an invention, and if and so long as the appropriate Service department considers that it ought to be kept secret, "acceptance" of the specification will not be followed by publication. Similar provisions apply to designs, and similar provisions apply to all inventions involving atomic energy, whether of military character or not.

Military inventions that the armed forces think good enough to use are just the ones they will want to keep secret. So the provisions giving inventors the right to be compensated for Crown use apply in such cases as if the patent were granted in the ordinary way. In addition, the Crown can if it likes compensate the inventor for the damage the secrecy does to him.

It would of course be useless to keep such inventions secret here if they were published abroad. For this reason, it is provided that no foreign patent may be applied for upon an invention made here, unless an application has first been filed here and six weeks have then elapsed without any direction being made that the invention should be kept secret.

PART III

TRADE MARKS AND UNFAIR COMPETITION

8

DIFFERENT DEGREES OF PROTECTION

Passing-off

Most European countries have some sort of general rule of law forbidding unfair competition. We have not: but most of the activities that such a rule would discourage run contrary to specific rules of English law. In particular we have a rule—and this is the subject of this Part of this book—forbidding the running of a business in such a way as to filch a competitor's trade. The limits of this rule will be discussed in later stages; all that need be said here is that it is in essence a rule to protect business goodwill. Lawyers have a rather definite concept of what they mean by goodwill: it is that characteristic of a business which renders it permanent, which distinguishes an established business from one newly formed. In order to protect business goodwill the law forbids any trader so to conduct his trade as to mislead customers into mistaking his goods for someone else's. Nor may he mislead customers into confusing his business as a whole with someone else's. It makes no difference whether it is other traders or the general public that are deceived; nor whether the deception is fraudulent or merely mistaken or accidental; nor how it is brought about. This sort of deception is known as " passing-off "; anyone who suffers financial loss as a result of it is entitled to bring an action in the courts, claiming compensation for his loss, and asking for an injunction against continuance of the deception. This is a powerful and effective remedy, provided only that the plaintiff is able to prove his case.

Where the case is clear on its face, or there is any serious indication that the defendant is dishonest, no difficulty arises, so long as the plaintiff moves quickly enough. He can ask for, and will be given a temporary injunction, putting a stop to the deception until the case can be tried—and that, almost always, is the end of the matter. The matter is settled and there is no need ever to have a full-scale trial. In cases that are less clear (and in cases where the plaintiff is too slow in taking action for the court to feel justified in anticipating the trial in this way) the difficulty of proof may be a serious one. So full trials of passing-off cases are rare. it is seldom possible to find anyone who has actually been deceived and will come and swear to it in court. The case must therefore be proved by showing that the circumstances are such that people are certain to be deceived sooner or later. This is not an easy task, and the most important reason for registering trade marks is to make it unnecessary.

PASSING-OFF AND REGISTRATION OF TRADE MARKS

It is a general rule that where there has been full registration of all trade marks, the sort of " passing-off " that involves imitation of trade marks or brand names can seldom occur without infringement of the trade mark registrations taking place too. Full registration of trade marks is not always easy or even possible; there are many legal pitfalls to be avoided. (Some of these are discussed in Chap. 11.) Where it is possible it enables the expensive and uncertain action for passing-off to be almost completely replaced by the cheaper and more reliable action for infringement of trade mark.

Passing-off and goodwill

In an action for passing-off the plaintiff must in practice prove that he has extensive enough goodwill for his goods to be recognised by members of the public; otherwise it will hardly be possible for people to be deceived when they come across similar goods put out by the defendants. It follows that the law of passing-off will protect established lines of goods of established businesses from imitation, but will not provide a shield behind which a new goodwill can be built up. Registration of a trade mark, on the other hand, is possible before the goods the mark is intended for are put on to the market at all. Since registration gives almost an absolute right to stop others from using that mark or a mark like it, goodwill can be built up behind the protection given by the Trade Marks Act.

Why people sue for passing-off

Why, if suing for infringement is so much easier, does anyone sue for passing-off? (Passing-off actions are the more numerous, in fact.) There are several reasons.

Many businesses do not keep their trade marks fully and validly registered, so that resort to a passing-off action may always be necessary to cover flaws in the trade mark position. Further, passing-off can occur in cases that have nothing at all to do with trade marks: by the use of a name for a new company that is misleadingly similar to that of an old one; by the marketing of goods whose get-up is the same (in everything but the wording on the package) as that of an old-established line; and so one.

Thus, in *Pullman (R. & J.) Ltd.* v. *Pullman* (1919) the defendant called his house by the name of the plaintiffs' factory and then used the similiarity of name to mislead the plaintiffs' customers into writing to him instead of to the plaintiffs: the court issued an injunction to stop the defendant from continuing to trade in that way. And in *Edge* v. *Niccolls* (1911) where the plaintiffs' goods carried no make's name but were very well known by the shape of the package, the defendants were prevented by an injunction from selling their goods in packages of that shape even with their own name on theirs. (Such cases are rare, however.)

" PART A " AND " PART B " MARKS

There are certain trade marks (those " registered in Part B of the register ") which have a degree of protection between that given by the " Part A " registrations, to which this chapter has so far referred, and that given by the law of passing-off. The plaintiff, in an action for infringement of his right to use one of these marks, is not required to prove that his goods are known to the public, and to that extent he is in the position of any registered trade mark owner; on the other hand, his action will fail, as a passing-off action will fail but an ordinary trade mark action will not, if the defendant can show that although he used the plaintiff's mark it was not used in a way that was likely to mislead the public. (This is almost certainly what section 5 of the Trade Marks Act 1938 means; but the language used could have other meanings: see *Broad & Co. Ltd.* v. *Graham Building Supplies Ltd.* (1969).) " Part B " registrations are for this reason less valuable than the ordinary " Part A "

Trade Marks and Unfair Competition

ones, but they are easier to get and not uncommon for that reason. A mark registered in Part B may, when substantial goodwill has been attached to it, later be registered also in Part A, although often people do not bother to do this; the conditions for such re-registration in Part A are further discussed in Chapter 10.

Infringement of " A " marks

The rights given by "Part A" registrations are much wider than mere protection of a trade mark from imitation in the ordinary sense (how much wider, nobody quite knows). It now seems settled that you cannot use another man's "Part A" mark to advertise your goods even in a comparative way. Thus it is probably an infringement to say in an advertisement "my camera is as good as a Kodak but half the price," whether this is true or not. The law of passing-off gives no rights of this sort. So if you merely say such things (*e.g.* in a shop, or in the form of a "voice over" on a television advertisement) and they are true, the owner of the mark cannot complain. You do not infringe because you have not used the mark visually and there is no passing-off. The position may be different if what is said is untrue—see Chapters 14 and 15.

LITIGATION CAUSED BY UNCERTAINTY

Where a registered trade mark has been infringed, this is usually clear. Furthermore, a direct search of the trade marks register will show what marks are there, and so indicate whether a new mark can safely be used or not. Most instances of trade mark infringement happen through pure inadvertence, and are stopped as soon as the proprietor of the mark complains. But just because passing-off may occur in cases where there is nothing on any register, and in cases where there is room for a real difference of opinion as to the legitimacy of what is being done, when litigation does occur it is more likely to be a passing-off action than an action for infringement. The failure to register a mark may only too easily have to be repaired by the courts. It is worth noting, though, that quite a lot of litigation arises from something for which the law gives no remedy: the spoiling of trade marks by getting too close to them— that is, the case where a trader picks a mark that, although not close enough to a competitor's actually to be mistaken for it, is yet close enough for the public (who have no real

Different Degrees of Protection

interest in these things, anyway) not to bother to prefer one brand to the other. This, in effect, is one way of saying to the public: "Mine is just as good."

PROTECTION UNDER THE CRIMINAL LAW

Business activities involving obvious fraud are sometimes more easily prevented by criminal prosecution under the Trade Descriptions Act, and similar enactments, than by an expensive and troublesome civil action; for instance, in cases where goods are adulterated before sale. Prosecution is, however, unwise unless the case is very clear—clearer than would be necessary for an ordinary action for an injunction and damages. See for example the "Spanish Champagne" case, where a civil action to stop sales of Spanish wine as "Spanish Champagne" succeeded (*Bollinger* v. *Costa Brava Wine Co.* (1961)) although a prosecution for it had already failed. This part of the criminal law is discussed in Chapter 15.

9

WHAT REGISTERED TRADE MARKS ARE FOR

INTRODUCTION

THIS chapter discusses, in more detail than the last, the rights of the registered proprietor of a trade mark. It refers primarily to marks "registered in Part A of the register"; the rules for "Part B" marks differ in certain ways which are discussed at the end of the chapter.

It is possible to resist any action for infringement of the rights given by registration of a trade mark by contending that the registration is invalid and asking for its cancellation. The rules deciding when a registration is valid and when it is not are discussed in Chapter 11. In the present chapter it will be assumed that all registrations are valid; in practice, most are.

THE GOODS FOR WHICH THE MARK IS REGISTERED

The registration of any person as proprietor of a trade mark in respect of any goods gives him the exclusive right to use that mark in relation to those goods. It gives him no right to stop the use of the mark on goods for which it is not registered. In practice, a mark ought to be registered for any goods its owner uses it on or intends to use it on, and also for all other goods of the same sort—that is, for what the law calls "goods of the same description," meaning roughly all goods that would be recognised by business people as belonging to the same trade. For detailed discussion of the words "of the same description," which occur in several parts of the Trade Marks Act, see especially "*Daiquiri Rum*" T.M. (1969).

Thus a trade mark used on three-hole razor-blades ought to be registered for all razor-blades and for razors as well. Most registrations are wider than this, but some firms make a practice of getting registrations that are far too narrow; for instance, "three-hole razor blades imported from Venezuela." This may or may not cover all goods on which the mark is likely to be used by its owner, so that he can put "registered trade mark" on his packet, and it will serve to stop other firms from actually registering marks for razor-blades that are too much like his; but it will be useless for preventing other firms from using his mark even on three-hole razor-blades, for it is most unlikely that they will import their goods from Venezuela. It will not even cover his own goods if he changes to a different source of supply or a different design of blade—as sooner or later he probably will. Just as bad would be registration for " a preparation of soap for use in shaving "; this would cover a shaving-cream made by the owner of the mark but would cover nothing else, possibly not even a different " preparation of soap for use in shaving " on which the mark was used by a competitor. Better a registration that is too wide: although it will be less effective or ineffective so far as the extra goods are concerned (this point is discussed later), it will, at least, protect the actual goods its owner uses it on. Too many traders, after carefully getting registration for a new trade mark they mean to use on some new product, then change their minds, and alter the mark, or use it for a different product, without a thought as to whether their registration will still cover what they are going to do.

INFRINGEMENT

(a) **By similar marks**

A trade mark will be infringed by the application to the wrong man's goods not only of that mark itself, but of any other mark so nearly resembling it as to be likely to be misleading. The public cannot be expected to remember every detail of the trade marks on the various articles they buy and use; if two marks are so alike that members of the public having a general recollection of the one and seeing the other are likely to confuse the two, the second mark will infringe a registration of the first. A long list of pairs of marks which the courts have found to be too close or not too close will be found in *Kerly*. As examples: " Pem Books " (for paperback books) was held to infringe " Pan Books "; " Pem " being a new mark. On the other hand, " Gala " for cosmetics was held not to infringe " Goya "; the two marks having both been used for some time. The decision rests, in the end, on what the court feels when it looks at the two marks; and in difficult cases, there is always a tendency to favour an established trade against a new entrant who as yet has built up no real goodwill—but to hesitate to interfere with a trade that has been going on for a considerable time without complaint. In borderline cases, the decision will depend on all those circumstances of the case that affect the likelihood of confusion; what sort of people the goods are sold to, for instance, and whether they are likely to be ordered over the telephone. It depends too on what particular features of the marks concerned stick in people's memory, so as to be the features that matter in determining whether two marks will be distinguished or confused: the "essential features" of the mark, as they are called. So also the court will consider what is the basic idea of the mark. Thus "Watermatic" was held to infringe "Aquamatic" (for toy pistols), the idea being the same although the sound is different; but "Kidax" (for clothing) was held not too close to "Daks," the court not accepting that "Kidax" would be confused with "kids' 'Daks.'" Now all this sort of thing depends on what evidence the court has as to conditions in the trade and the way the businesses concerned are carried on, something hard to forecast before the case is heard. In general, though, it is necessary only to look at the two marks to see whether there is an infringement, or no infringement, or perhaps a borderline case. As we said before, this certainty means that litigation is seldom needed to settle disputes. One general rule is that legitimate use of one validly registered trade mark will never infringe another, so that a business which makes a practice of applying to register all trade marks for the right goods before using them is unlikely to run into difficulties over infringements of other people's marks.

Unless there is a note on the register limiting a trade mark to particular colours, it will not be affected by a change in colour. (On this point the law of England is different from that of some foreign countries.) If a word is registered in block capitals, the registration will be infringed by a use of that word in lettering of any sort; the converse is, however, not necessarily true. It is not possible to avoid infringement by adding other matter to a mark, so that if company A have registered a mark and company B use it on their own goods, they will infringe A's rights, however different the get-up of their goods from A's, and however prominently their own name appears on the packets or labels. This absolute character of the rights given by trade mark registration is essentially different from the right to prevent misleading imitations by an action for "passing-off."

(b) Acts constituting infringement

It was indicated in the last chapter that the rights of

What Registered Trade Marks are For

the registered owner of a trade mark go far beyond simply preventing others from using his mark as a trade mark on their goods. Just how far beyond is not clear. The leading case on this point, *Bismag* v. *Amblins* (*Chemists*) (1940), was about a catalogue published by the defendants, who were a firm of chemists. After explaining that their own products were at least as good as the nationally advertised brands, only cheaper, they set out in parallel columns a list on the left of widely advertised proprietary medicines with an analysis and the price of each, and a list on the right of their own corresponding products with identical analyses and much lower prices. The lay-out was such as to emphasise the correspondence between similar items in the two columns, and many of the proprietary brands in the left-hand column were referred to by registered trade marks. The Court of Appeal held that these registered marks were used " in relation " to the defendant's goods listed in the right-hand column as well as to the corresponding items on the left; the trade marks were consequently infringed. It is never safe for a trader to use any word or design, resembling anyone else's trade mark, either on goods which do not already lawfully carry that mark or in an advertisement relating to goods that do not lawfully carry that mark; and if the Court of Appeal interpreted the law correctly (the House of Lords doubted this in *Aristoc* v. *Rysta* (1945)) it is not safe to use such a mark in any context, unless it refers exclusively to goods lawfully carrying the mark.

To infringe, the mark must be used " in the course of trade," and must be written or printed: speaking a mark is not infringement, although it may involve passing-off. Also, the mark must be used in some sort of trade-mark sense. It should be noted, however, that there will be no infringement unless the registration covers the " wrong " goods; for instance, if " Clippo " were registered for " three-hole razor-blades imported from Venezuela," it would be an infringement to label other Venezuelan blades " better than Clippo," but it would be no infringement to put the same statement on blades made in England. This is a typical example of the complications caused by registering trade marks too narrowly.

(c) Restricting use by others of a registered mark

The owner of a trade mark is allowed in certain cases to extend still further the rights given him by registration: he may prevent purchasers of goods carrying the mark (unless

Trade Marks and Unfair Competition

they remove entirely from those goods the mark and the maker's name) from altering the packing or get-up of the goods, or the mark or any lettering associated with it. Further, a purchaser may be prevented from using the mark on the goods concerned after their condition has changed or been modified. Thus it could be made an infringement (if the owner of the trade mark wanted) to sell a second-hand or rebuilt typewriter under the original trade mark; or to sell goods loose under the trade mark where they were originally put up in packets; or to remove a trade mark which indicates the quality of a particular line without removing all markings that connect the line with a particular manufacturer. The imposition of this sort of restriction calls for a written agreement covering the actual goods concerned, and is not often done. Where the owner of a trade mark has himself used his mark, or allowed it to be used, on his own goods, and there is no such agreement covering the goods, it can never be an infringement to sell them under that mark—although it may amount to passing-off, see *Westinghouse* v. *The Varsity Eliminator* (1935). To use a mark on goods with which the owner of the mark has no trade connection is theoretically still infringement, even if it is done with his consent. If this happens on a considerable scale the registration of the mark will become invalid in most cases; but there could conceivably be cases when the registration will stay valid and an action for infringement will be possible. The question of validity in such cases is further discussed in Chapter 11.

EXCEPTIONS TO THE GENERAL INFRINGEMENT RULES

(a) **Accessories and spares**

Accessories and spares can, if necessary, be sold by reference to the trade marks used on the goods they are spares or accessories for, provided care is taken not to suggest they are made by or connected with the owners of the marks—there is a difference between "spares for Leyland" and "Leyland spares"—and provided it is reasonably necessary. Thus in the photographic trade, it is customary and proper to sell accessories, such as lenses, by reference to the brands of camera they fit; there is, after all, no other sensible way of describing them. But film is not normally sold in that sort of way, because only in special cases is it necessary to name the camera: there are standard code numbers which in most cases will give purchasers all the information they need.

(b) Use of one's own name

Honest use by a trader of his own name, or the name of his place of business, cannot be an infringement of trade mark; this applies to trading companies as well as to individuals. Furthermore, a trader who causes no more confusion than is inseparable from the use of his own name will not be guilty of passing-off. (He may have to avoid putting his name actually on his goods.) But the name must be genuinely his own (his full name, if necessary); and if he uses it to deceive he may be held to be passing-off even though the Act gives him a defence to an action for infringement. Nor may a man who forms a company lend his name to it, so as to give it a special right to use the name.

(c) Honest use as a description

A trade mark cannot be infringed by an honest description of goods, where people reading the description will not think of it as referring to the owner of the mark or his goods. This is not a point that often arises, except with those rare registered trade marks (like "Yale" for locks or "Vaseline" for petroleum jelly) that the public use as the common name for the goods. Obviously, a trader who habitually uses other people's trade marks for his own goods is likely to land in trouble in the end, notwithstanding this provision of the Act; but it covers exceptional cases where a customer needs to have the position explained, and also occasional genuine slips.

(d) Old established marks

Registration of a trade mark will not enable its owner to stop anyone who was using it before registration (and has used it ever since) from going on using it, unless the registered owner started using it first. In each case only use on the particular sort of goods concerned counts. Suppose, for instance, a trade mark is registered by the A Co. for tobacco generally. It later turns out that the B Co. have for some time been using a mark very like it on pipe tobacco. The A Co. can stop the sale of this pipe tobacco if and only if they or their predecessors in business used their mark on pipe tobacco before the B Co. started using theirs. The A Co. may have been using their mark on cigarettes for many years, but this is irrelevant. On the other hand, the B Co.'s rights are limited to pipe tobacco; they cannot extend the use of their mark to cover cigarettes, unless they can get it registered for cigarettes (as to which see the next chapter).

Trade Marks and Unfair Competition

Such a state of affairs ought, however, never to be allowed to arise; both companies ought to have applied to register their marks earlier; while the B Co. ought to have opposed the A Co.'s application for registration, so as to cut pipe tobacco out of the list of goods covered by it.

Who Should be Sued for Infringement

It is in practice very rare for any trader to infringe a registered trade mark. If infringement does occur, an action to enforce the rights of the owner of the mark may be brought either against the person who applied the mark to the goods in the first place (or imported them, if they were marked abroad), or against anyone who has subsequently traded in them. Each subsequent trader, however, will usually have the right to bring into the action as a " third party " the person who sold the goods to him, so that in the last resort whoever marked or imported the goods will usually be liable for the whole of the damages, and if he has the money to pay them there will often be commercial advantages in bringing the action against him only. Dealers lower down the line are seldom sued unless the owner of the mark cannot discover who made or imported the goods (suing the dealer may be one way of finding this out), or the dealers themselves have large stocks of falsely-marked goods.

Contested Actions

The defendant in an action for infringement of trade mark can (and if he fights the case at all usually does) claim by way of defence that the registration of the mark is invalid, and ask the court to cancel it. The case is likely to be lengthy, complicated and expensive, though not as expensive as a passing-off action would be. If the validity of the registration is disputed and is upheld by the court the owner of the the mark may ask the court for a " certificate of validity " for the registration (just as in a patent case, see Chap. 5). In practice, the certificate acts as a warning to the trade that this particular mark is too firmly established to be safely challenged.

Special Rules for Part B Marks

When a trade mark is registered in Part B of the register, there is generally no right to sue for infringement if it can be proved that whatever has been done will not confuse or mislead the public. In particular, cases of infringement of the " this is as good as ' Vaseline ' " type can never occur with " Part B " marks if the statement made is true.

NOTE: TESTS FOR INFRINGEMENT

It is useful to compare the test of whether two marks are too close to one another, for the purpose of infringement of A and B marks, with the standard tests for registrability set out in the next Chapter. For an A mark, the test is almost that under section 12: Is there any normal and fair use of the two marks concerned, on the goods concerned, that would lead to confusion? Thus " get-up " is irrelevant. For a B mark, we look for confusion between any normal and fair use of the plaintiff's (registered) mark, and the actual use the defendant is making of his (allegedly infringing) mark. The test for passing-off is similar to that for B infringement: we consider the actual use the defendant is making of his mark, having regard to the reputation acquired by the plaintiff's mark. (The burden of proof is of course different in these various cases.)

It should be remembered that although this is probably what the section of the Act about Part B marks means, the language could have other meanings too (see *Broad & Co.* v. *Graham Building Supplies* (1969)).

10

HOW TO REGISTER A TRADE MARK

INTRODUCTION

THIS chapter explains what sort of thing can be registered as a trade mark, gives an outline of the procedure for registration, discusses the conditions for registration to be possible, and explains when other people's applications can be successfully opposed. As before, the bulk of the chapter deals with Part A registrations; Part B registrations are different in ways discussed at the end of the chapter.

WHAT IS A " MARK "?

Almost anything changing the appearance of the goods can be a " mark ": coloured threads woven into a hose, for instance (*Reddaway's Application* (1914)) or even the colouring of pellets inside a part-transparent drug capsule (*Smith Kline & French's Applications* (1975)).

REGISTRABLE MARKS

To be registrable, a mark must be in use or intended for use as a trade mark, and must be distinctive.

(a) Mark must be used as a trade mark

A mark is not used as a trade mark, and so is not registrable, unless it is used to indicate a " connection in the course of trade " between the owner of the mark and his goods. It does not matter what sort of trade connection; manufacturers, dealers, importers, even people who never own the goods, can all have trade marks. In the case of accessories, for instance, the maker of the article they are to be used with may apply a trade mark to them to show he approves their use with his goods; " Kodak Film " might mean (though in fact it does not) film made and sold by an entirely different concern and approved for use with " Kodak " cameras. But there must be some trade connection between the owner of the mark and the goods before they get into the hands of consumers; otherwise, the mark is not used as a trade mark. As an extreme example, it was decided that a mark applied by a company whose business was the repairing of stockings, to the stockings they repaired, was not a trade mark and so could not be registered (*Aristoc* v. *Rysta* (1945)).

(b) Marks must be distinctive

The most important requirement for a registrable trade mark is that it must be distinctive, in the sense of being suitable for distinguishing goods with which its owner has some trade connection from the goods of other concerns. (It must also be sufficiently unlike other people's trade marks for the public not to confuse them; but that is rather a different point and will be discussed later on.) For the purpose of deciding the question of distinctiveness the law divides marks into three sorts: those which will be presumed to be distinctive; those which can never be distinctive; and those which come in between, that is they are refused registration unless it is proved that they have become distinctive in use.

(i) *Marks presumed to be distinctive*

The most important of these are invented or fanciful words, and designs. These are only refused registration if they are proved to be in common use in the trade concerned or are too like existing marks.

(ii) *Marks which can never be distinctive*

These are marks that anyone might want to use, such as names of countries or substantial towns; words that are mere laudatory epithets—or words that sound exactly the same as any of these. The clearest case on the point is *Yorkshire Copper Work's Application* (1954) in which, even though the applicants offered to show that the mark "Yorkshire" meant their pipe fitting to 100 per cent. of those in the trade, registration was refused, the House of Lords saying that such distinctiveness was merely transient in the sense that another manufacturer might wish to set up a pipe fitting plant in Yorkshire. Other cases are "Electrix" (for electric vacuum cleaners—it sounds like "Electrics," *Electrix Ltd.'s Application* (1959)) and "Perfection" (for soap, *Crosfield's Application* (1909)). Further examples are in *Kerly*.

(iii) *Marks whose distinctiveness must be proved*

In between these extremes comes a large class of marks that are unregistrable when newly adopted, but can become registrable when use over a sufficient period has made them familiar as trade marks. When application for registration of such a mark is made, the Registrar has to balance its inherent unsuitability for registration against the evidence produced by the applicant that the mark has become distinctive. How much evidence is needed depends of course on the particular mark; some (very rare surnames, for instance, or the names of obscure foreign towns) may be almost inherently registrable; some (common surnames, larger towns) almost totally unregistrable. Words that come rather close to describing the goods come into this category, as well as geographical names and surnames. As an example, the word " Livron " was accepted for registration for use on a medicine containing liver and iron, but it was taken off the register again on the ground that it was the name of a small town in France where another manufacturer of drugs had a factory (*Boots' T.M.* (1937)). Personal names are in much the same position as surnames alone (although the signature of the applicant for registration or a predecessor in business of his comes into class (i) above). Names of companies must also be proved to be distinctive (unless they are " represented in a special or particular manner," when again they fall into class (i)). Initials are very hard to get registered, because they are shared by many people and companies; only the very best-known companies are allowed to register them (B.P., for instance, and E.M.I.) and even then registration is usually with some sort of pictorial arrangement or " device." Further examples of this " in between " class are " Trakgrip " which was registered for motor tyres on proof that only the applicants used it and that other traders would not be likely to want to use it to describe their own goods (*Dunlop's Application* (1942)); and " Sheen " for cotton, on evidence of widespread use by the applicants (*J. & P. Coats Ltd.'s Application* (1936)).

(c) Distinctive in practice

In all these matters, the fundamental question is: would registration embarrass other traders? Is the matter constituting the mark something that other traders might reasonably want to employ, otherwise than for dishonest purposes in describing, or advertising their goods? If so, it should not be registered; if not, it may be registrable.

When a mark has been used for some time on a large scale, however, a position is likely to arise where it is so

How to Register a Trade Mark

well known as one trader's mark that no honest competitor would use it. At that stage, a mark that was unregistrable before comes close to registrability; and in the end, all but the sort of marks we have mentioned as being totally unregistrable will be allowed registration. However, it would seldom be wise for a business to use an unregistrable mark hoping to register it later. The risk of failure is too great, even in those rare cases where there is a good chance of monopolising an existing demand. Most of the cases of attempts at late registration have been cases where trade mark questions were not fully considered when the goodwill was built up; and only too often the attempt has failed. (The *Electrix* story, at the end of Chap. 11, shows how this sort of thing can happen.) Sometimes, though, for a short-lived product, it may make sense to pick a mark too descriptive ever to become registrable during the product's life; the descriptive character of the mark can make it easier for the public to recognise.

THE APPLICATION

Application to register a trade mark must be made to the Registrar of Trade Marks (except in the case of registrations of marks for cotton and metal goods, which can, if preferred, be applied for instead in Manchester and Sheffield respectively). The Registrar's office is at the Patent Office, which he administers under the alternative title of Comptroller-General of Patents, Designs and Trade Marks. The office is part of the Department of Trade, which also has certain direct responsibilities in relation to trade marks. Applications are normally made by trade mark agents, who are usually but not always patent agents too. The application fee is £20, with a further £30 for registration if the application succeeds. After that the renewal fees are £73 (with penalties for lateness in paying), payable after seven years' registration and payable again every 14 years thereafter.

(a) The class of goods

Goods are divided into 34 classes for trade-mark purposes, and on those comparatively rare occasions when registration of a mark is wanted for goods in more than one class, separate applications are needed and the resulting registrations are treated as separate. " Registration " in this book will normally mean " registration for a selection of

Trade Marks and Unfair Competition

goods all in one class." Typical classes are: machines and machine-tools; fuels, industrial oils and lubricants; vehicles; clothing; games and playthings; wines, spirits and liqueurs.

In most classes, registrations for all goods in the class will be allowed by the Registrar, and where this is so, that should be the normal form of registration; for reasons, some of which were pointed out in the last chapter, too wide a registration is better than too narrow. The applicant is only entitled, however, to a registration covering those goods on which he is using or intends to use the mark, and goods " of the same description " (for the meanings of this expression see the beginning of the last chapter). A wider registration than this may be refused by the Registrar, and if obtained may be pruned down later on.

A registration as wide as the whole class, or even covering " goods of the same description," may be difficult, for the mark may contain wording that would be misleading if applied to other goods in the same class or of the same description: a word suggesting "nylon," for instance, applied to cotton shirts. Yet the owner of the mark must try to cover such cases: for that sort of misleading use would be the most damaging sort of infringement. Similar problems arise with marks implying a particular place of origin (*e.g.* a mark including the Venezuelan flag). Usually, the Registrar will allow registration on condition the mark is only used so as not to mislead (as with " Maltesers," registered on condition that the goods it was used on should contain malt); if not, it is sometimes possible to get over the difficulty by registering a " series " of marks, alike except for small variations making them suitable for use on the different goods or on goods from the different countries concerned. Otherwise, only in exceptional cases should a registration narrower than the " description " be asked for, and even then care should be taken to include spare parts and accessories.

(b) Who must apply

The application must be made by the person, firm or company actually using or intending to use the trade mark. If the registration is obtained by someone not intending to use the mark the registration may be invalid, and may remain invalid even if the mark is subsequently handed over to the right owner. Thus, where a mark is in use by a private company on its goods, an application to register it in the name of (say) the chief shareholder would be refused by the Registrar if he knew the true facts; if it were so registered the registration would be invalid, and even if the Registrar could be persuaded to register an assignment to the company the registration might still be invalid. There are, however, two exceptions to this rule. The first is that if the mark is to be used by a company not yet formed, it may be registered by anyone who intends to assign it to the company in due course; but it must be so assigned within 12 months or the registration will be cancelled. The second exception arises in connection with "registered users" and will be referred to in the next chapter. There is a third, unofficial exception, that it does not much matter in whose name a mark is originally registered, provided it gets into the right hands before any use is made of it; but it is much better not to rely on this exception and to register correctly in the first place.

(c) Joint applicants

There may be two or more applicants if and only if they are all going to have a trade connection with all the goods sold under the mark. For instance, a foreign manufacturer and the sole importer of his goods may register a mark in their joint names; but if some of the goods on which the mark is used are going to be manufactured in this country such a registration will be invalid. If some of the goods are to be made by one manufacturer and some by another a joint registration will almost certainly be invalid. The difficult problem of finding arrangements that can be used in such cases without making the registration invalid is discussed further in the next chapter. Joint registrations, however, should be avoided, unless it is essential for commercial reasons that two independent companies should both retain control over the mark.

(d) Objections by the Registrar

The Registrar may object to an application on the ground that the mark concerned is inherently not distinctive; may demand evidence or better evidence that it is distinctive; may object that the specification of goods that the registration is to cover is too wide; may object that the mark is immoral, illegal, improper, scandalous or misleading; or may object (after searching the register for similar marks) that the mark is too like others on the register or in use. The applicant may meet these objections by withdrawing his application or altering it (changing the specification of goods to be covered, asking for a "Part B" instead of a "Part A" registration and so on), or may demand a "hearing"; that is, the right to go to the Patent Office and argue the case before the Registrar or one of his senior assistants. The actual arguing, in practice, is done by the agent or by counsel.

If at the hearing the Registrar is not persuaded, the applicant may appeal to the High Court or (if he prefers) to the Department of Trade. Alternatively, the applicant may submit a written case to the Registrar instead of asking for a hearing, and may appeal as before if the Registrar does not change his mind. Appeals to the Department of Trade are referred to Queen's Counsel with special trade-mark experience for decision; which is cheaper and may be quicker too.

About half the applications for registration fail altogether. About one in 10 applications for a "Part A" mark, results in a "Part B" registration after argument with the Registrar; that is how most (over 80 per cent.) of "Part B" registrations come about.

(e) Acceptance and advertisement

If and when the Registrar has no further objection to mark, the application will be accepted and the intention to register it will be advertised in *The Trade Marks Journal*. If the Registrar is especially doubtful of a mark, or it is the sort of mark that cannot be registered unless it is proved to be distinctive, he may advertise the application (and so ask for oppositions) before accepting it. In either case the mark will not be actually registered until long enough after the advertisement for anyone who wants to oppose the application to do so. The Registrar will allow the applicant and any opponent to argue the case before him if they wish and the loser can appeal to the High Court. If there is no successful opposition, the Registrar will register the mark unless the Department of Trade tells him not to.

(f) Opposition

Anyone may oppose an application, either on the ground that the Registrar ought not to have accepted it or on the ground that the registration would be invalid if it were made. The usual reason for opposition is that the new mark is too similar to a mark the opponents are using or have registered or hope to use or register. (Once they have decided to oppose the application at all, however, opponents

How to Register a Trade Mark

will naturally raise any other objections to it that they can find.) For instance, an application to register "Nuvol" was successfully opposed by the owners of "Nujol" (*McDowell's Application* (1927)), while an application to register "Ovax" was unsuccessfully opposed by the owners of "Hovis" ("*Ovax*" case (1946); see below). Or the owner of a series of marks having a common feature may object to an application by anyone else to register a mark that might look like another member of the series; for instance, a manufacturer wishing to distinguish his goods by the name of the city where they are made, and unable to persuade the Registrar to accept that name as a trade mark, may produce much the same effect by registering a number of marks containing that name ("Bombay Buttercup," "Bombay Bombshell" and so on), and at the same time opposing any application by anyone else to register any mark containing it.

Oppositions are often bitterly fought, not only by opponents (who have often much to lose, since the new registration might reduce the value of their existing goodwill), but also by applicants although (as was pointed out above) the goodwill in a new trade mark can seldom be worth the legal costs involved. The opposition proceedings may even, in the course of successive appeals, reach the House of Lords, which will involve the loser in costs running into tens of thousands of pounds.

More About Oppositions

(a) The main ground—similarity of marks

The main ground of opposition, that of similarity to existing marks, may be put in two ways: first, that the familiarity of the public with existing marks (registered or unregistered) is such that they would be seriously misled or confused by the use of the mark whose registration is now asked for; and, secondly, that the new mark, and some mark already registered, could be so used by their respective owners (without going outside the terms of their respective registrations) as to confuse or mislead the public. These two objections are by no means the same. The first will not apply if the older mark has not in fact acquired any public reputation and in particular if it has never been used at all. The second will not apply if the older mark is unregistered.

(b) The burden is on the applicant

It is the responsibility of an applicant for registration to

Trade Marks and Unfair Competition

satisfy the Registrar that if his mark is registered and used no confusion will arise in either of these two ways. If he cannot so satisfy the Registrar (or the court on appeal from the Registrar), his application will fail.

The Registrar will sometimes accept an application, where the only objection is the existence on the register of a similar mark whose owner consents to the new application; but this will only be done in cases where no serious confusion is to be expected. The advertisement of such an application will state that it is made " by consent."

If there are other similar marks on the register belonging to the applicant, this will, of course, be no objection to registration, but the new mark will be " associated " with the old ones; the main effect of this is that they can never belong to different owners, unless the Registrar cancels the association.

(c) The " Ovax " Case

The *" Ovax "* case (*Smith, Hayden & Co.'s Application* (1946)) illustrates these points. The mark " Hovis " had been registered since 1895 for " Substances used as food or as ingredients in food," and had been used on a very large scale though apparently only on flour and bread. Hovis Ltd., the proprietors of " Hovis," also owned a mark " Ovi " registered for much the same variety of goods, but there was no evidence that this mark had ever been used at all. The case concerned an application (opposed by Hovis Ltd.) to register the mark " Ovax " for " A cereal preparation for use as an improver and moistening agent in making cakes." The Registrar allowed the application and Hovis Ltd. appealed to the court. Here is the test the court had to apply—as slightly altered by the House of Lords (*Bali T.M.* (1969)):

" In these circumstances, the questions for my decision under the two sections of the Act have been formulated, and I think accurately formulated, as follows: (a) (under section 11) 'Having regard to the use of the name " Hovis," is the court satisfied that the mark applied for, if used in a normal and fair manner in connection with any goods covered by the registration proposed, will not be reasonably likely to cause deception and confusion amongst a substantial number of persons? '; (b) (under section 12) ' Assuming user by Hovis Ltd. of their marks " Hovis " and " Ovi " in a normal and fair manner for any of the goods covered by the registrations of those marks (and including particularly goods also covered by the proposed registration of the mark " Ovax ") is the court satisfied that there will be no reasonable likelihood of deception or confusion among a substantial number of persons if Smith, Hayden & Co. Ltd. also use their mark " Ovax " normally and fairly in respect of any goods covered by their proposed registration? '

It is clear that the onus lies upon Smith, Hayden & Co. Ltd., as applicants for registration, of satisfying the court that a negative answer should be given to both questions, regard being had to the range of goods covered by the proposed registration."

It will be seen that the second question covers a wider field of inquiry than the first, so that if the second can be answered " Yes," the first need seldom be asked.

In the " *Ovax* " case, the court was satisfied that there was no such likelihood of confusion or deception and allowed " Ovax " to be registered.

(d) Other examples

In *Jellinek's Application* (1946) the applicant sought to register for shoe polish a mark containing the word " Panda " and a panda's picture, and was opposed by the owners of a mark registered for boots and shoes and containing the word " Panda " with a different picture of a panda. The opposition was based on both the grounds explained above. It failed on the first ground, because the opponents had not yet actually used their mark at the time when the applicants applied for theirs, so that there was no reputation among the public which could make use of the new mark misleading. It failed on the second ground because the court held that shoes and shoe polish are not goods " of the same description " (that is, they belong to two different trades: see the beginning of the last chapter); and when this is so, the second ground of objection does not apply. Again, an application to register " Jardex " for disinfectants was opposed by the owners of a registration of " Jardox " for an extract of meat: *Edward's Application* (1946). The second ground of objection did not arise (since meat extract and disinfectant are not goods of the same description), but the opponents' meat extract had been sold to hospitals on a considerable scale and the applicants' disinfectant was poisonous and, in view of the disastrous consequences that might result from confusion in a hospital between the two products the application was rejected on the first ground. The Registrar also pointed out that it was his duty, under the general discretion he possesses to refuse all objectionable trade-mark applications, to refuse to register any mark whose use might so endanger the public.

REGISTRATION IN CASES WHERE CONFUSION IS LIKELY

In special circumstances, a mark may be registered notwithstanding a likelihood of confusion. In such cases the Registrar may impose limitations on registration or conditions on use, so as to minimise the danger of misleading the public. For instance, a mark might be registered for goods to be exported only, or only for goods to be sold in particular areas in this country. In *Bass* v. *Nicholson* (1932) there was an application to register for bitter beer a mark including a triangle; the application was opposed by Bass, who had a very well-known trade mark for pale ale and beer consisting of a triangle, usually but by no means always used in the form of a red triangle. The Registrar allowed the application, but only for a white triangle (white being the only colour the applicants had used); the case ultimately reached the House of Lords, who upheld this decision but further limited the registration by excluding bottled beer from it.

Where a confusing mark is registered because of special circumstances, the Registrar has special powers further to reduce the danger of confusion by limiting the registrations of marks already registered so as to prevent their use on goods or in areas where they are not already used. These powers to cut down existing registrations are discussed in the next chapter.

The " special circumstance " usually relied on as justifying the presence on the register of two conflicting marks is what is called " honest concurrent use ": that the mark whose registration is now asked for has been in actual use for some years. In the " *Triangle* " case, for instance, the applicants had been using their mark since before the Trade Marks Register was opened. The mark has to have been used honestly, and less than some seven years of reasonably large-scale use is unlikely to justify registration.

MORE ABOUT CONFUSION

The insistence on avoiding any likelihood of confusing or misleading the public runs through the whole of trade mark law. The confusion that may arise from the simultaneous use of two similar marks is only one instance. Another instance occurred when "Orlwoola" was registered as a trade mark for various articles including clothing. The Court of Appeal had to decide whether it ought to remain registered. Lord Justice Fletcher Moulton said:

> "This case presents no difficulty. It is in substance a case of registration of the words 'All wool,' grotesquely mis-spelt, as a trade mark for textile fabrics. . . . If the goods are made wholly of wool, the words are natural and almost necessary description of them. If they are not made wholly of wool it is a misdescription that is so certain to deceive that its use can hardly be otherwise than fraudulent. In either case the words are utterly unfit for registration as a trade mark": ("*Orlwoola*" T.M.s (1909)).

REMOVAL FROM THE REGISTER

After a mark has been registered, it can be removed, either by application to the Registrar with appeal to the court or by direct application to the court in two broad classes of case, namely where there was something wrong with the original registration and where something has gone wrong after registration. In theory the original registration of a "Part B" mark always remains open to attack, but the original registration of "Part A" marks is protected to a certain degree after seven years: see below.

It is harder to get a mark taken off the register than to prevent its registration; if there is any doubt about the case no action will be taken, so that an unregistered mark will stay off the register and a registered mark will stay on. Furthermore, if the objections to registration have gone in the meantime—for example, if a mark that was not distinctive has since become so—the court will probably refuse to strike the mark off.

It is now settled that the classes of case where a mark can be removed for post-registration defects are limited to those set out in the Act; there is no general removal power ("*GE*" T.M. (1973)). These cases are more fully discussed in the next chapter. They consist of non-use, deceptiveness arising through the fault of the proprietor, and certain types of descriptiveness.

When the mark has been registered in Part A for seven years, the question whether it ought to have been registered in the first place can only be reopened if registration was obtained by fraud; or if the mark was illegal, immoral, improper or scandalous; or if use of the mark would be likely to confuse or mislead the public by reason of previous use of some similar mark, not merely by reason of the presence of a similar mark on the register. This last ground can be important; but in general a seven-year-old " Part A " registration is safe enough provided its owner avoids the pitfalls discussed in the next chapter.

DEFENSIVE REGISTRATION OF TRADE MARKS

The law does not discourage the use of similar trade marks by firms in quite different trades; it has already been pointed out that a mark cannot be validly registered in the ordinary way so as to cover goods belonging to a different trade from that in which the mark is actually to be used. (It is quite hard enough nowadays to find a satisfactory trade mark without worrying about marks used in other trades.) Some trade marks, however, are so well known that members of the public seeing them on quite different goods would be likely to suppose that those goods were connected with the company that normally used the mark. Trade marks of this sort, if and only if the mark consists of " an invented word or words " (see below), may be " defensively " registered for any goods to which their reputation extends in this way, but getting such registrations is not easy: see *Ferodo's Application* (1945). A " defensive " registration cannot be attacked on the ground that the mark is not used for goods of the sort concerned. It can, however, be attacked on the ground that defensive registration is no longer justified; that is, on the ground that the mark no longer possesses the qualification stated above for defensive registration covering the particular goods concerned. Except for this difference, a defensive registration is equivalent to an ordinary one; but the difference is important. In an infringement action based on a defensive registration the defendant will be able to raise, by an attack on validity, the whole question of how well known the mark is. The action will then resemble to some extent the " passing-off " actions mentioned in Chapter 8 (and discussed further in Chap. 13). The same attack on validity can be made if the owner of the defensive registration opposes an application by someone else to register a similar mark; with the result that if the opposition proceedings are seriously contested they will take much the same course as if the defensive registration

How to Register a Trade Mark

did not exist and the opposition were based purely on the alternative ground of the public reputation enjoyed by the earlier mark.

Since one of the main objects of registering trade marks is to avoid these arguments about reputations, defensive registrations are to some extent less valuable than ordinary ones. Furthermore, it has been held that conflict with a defensive registration is avoided by even slight changes in the word concerned (*Eastex Application* (1947); "Eastex" not too close to "Lastex"). On the other hand, the mere presence of a mark on the register will discourage most potential infringers, especially if they cannot be sure of proving that it is invalid; and most applicants for registration will hesitate before trying to prove that a well-known trade mark is not as well known as it was (or as the Registrar thought it was, when he made the defensive registration). Further, unless a defensive registration is actually invalid, it has the same absolute force as an ordinary one.

The right to obtain a defensive registration is strictly confined to the owners of marks consisting of invented words. Thus, to quote examples of actual trade marks, it would be possible to obtain defensive registrations for "Kodak," but never for "June" or "Blue Orchid" (which are ordinary English words), nor for surnames such as "Parker" or "Bentley," or for devices such as the "Homepride flourgrader" or the Bass triangle which are not words at all, or for initials such as "B.P." "Portmanteau" words such as "Sardovy"—"sardine" and "anchovy"—mostly count as invented: mere mis-spellings (like "Orlwoola") do not.

"PART B" MARKS

The rules for applications to register trade marks in Part B of the register are the same as for Part A, except that the standard of distinctiveness is lower. A "Part B" mark need not be distinctive when registered, so long as it is capable of becoming distinctive in use. So "Ustikon" has been registered for stick-on rubber soles: *Davis* v. *Sussex Rubber Co.* (1927). Marks such as "Yorkshire," that are totally unregistrable in Part A, are not registrable in Part B either: for they can never become truly distinctive. In theory, indeed, with any mark that can be registered only upon exceptionally strong evidence that it has become distinctive, there ought seldom to be a case where the evidence justifies registration in Part B without equally justifying registration in Part A. Where there is an objection to registration on the ground of closeness to an existing mark, too, it is theoretically little easier to get a B than an A registration. In practice, however, it seems that a mark that for any reason is just on the borderline of registrability in Part A will usually be accepted by the Registrar for Part B. This is what Part B is for.

After a " Part B " mark has been used to any considerable extent it ought to have become distinctive in the true sense so as to be registrable in Part A. As soon as this is the case the owner of the mark can, and normally should, make a fresh application to register it, this time in Part A. Not only does the change give the owner greater rights to stop infringement and simplify the bringing of infringement actions, it also helps to make his ownership more secure; for the rule protecting seven-year-old registrations does not apply to " Part B " marks.

There is one purpose for which a " Part B " registration is as good as any other. Some countries require trade marks registered for use by British firms to have been previously registered here, but do not distinguish between the two parts of our register. This was the main reason why Part B was established, and it is a pity that registration in Part B was so narrowly restricted. There is a need for a Part C, containing a mere record of actual marks in use, so as to enable foreign registrations to be based on them.

In any case, a " Part B " registration is much better than no registration at all.

11

PITFALLS IN TRADE MARK LAW

INTRODUCTION

THE purpose of this chapter is to explain what precautions should be taken to keep a trade mark registration valid. It applies both to " Part A " and to " Part B " marks.

The law on this subject is not in a satisfactory state. It was recognised before 1938 that the technicalities of the law made it sometimes very difficult to preserve the validity of trade marks, and the 1938 Act includes important changes intended to make preservation easier. But even now the effect of the Act is by no means clear, so that it is not always safe to assume that the old difficulties have gone. Furthermore, some other countries remain more rigid in outlook, so that marks used on some exported goods have to be handled according to the old rules. By and large, in most countries, it is possible somehow or other to do anything with a trade mark that can be done here, but there are exceptions.

THE OLD RULE: —THE MARK MUST NOT MISLEAD

The basic rule of the old law was that a trade mark must never be allowed to be misleading. It followed that the owner of a mark must never allow anyone else to use it; for it ought to be associated in the public mind with his goods only, and if it were used on anyone else's goods this must mislead the public either as to whose goods they were or as to who was the owner of the mark. It followed, also, that a mark could never be transferred from one owner to another except together with the whole goodwill of the business in which it was used; for the mark ought to be associated in the public mind with that business, so that any use of it by a new owner must be misleading. If the business was split up or came to an end, its trade marks were considered to be abandoned. Nor could the owner of a trade mark change the nature of his trade connection with the goods it was used on; if, for instance, the mark belonged to a manufacturer, and he started using it on goods made by someone else and merely distributed by him, the public would think he was still the manufacturer and so be misled. In this country these subsidiary rules have been largely abolished by the 1938 Act; but the mark will be invalid either if it was likely to deceive or cause confusion at the time when it was registered or if it has become likely to cause confusion since that date by reason of some blameworthy act of the registered proprietor (" *GE* " *Trade Mark* (1973)).

CHANGING THE WAY THE MARK IS USED

Consider, for instance, a change in type of trade connection, and consider as an example the manufacturer who starts using his mark on goods made for him by someone else. The 1938 Act says that such a change in the way the mark is used is not to be considered as sufficient in itself to make the mark misleading. The difficulty arises if the public are in fact misled—if they do in fact believe that the marked goods are still made by the same people. Does this make the registration of the mark invalid? Probably not, but there is no certainty about it. The only really safe course is to advertise widely the nature of the new arrangements; but few proprietors do.

CHANGE IN OWNERSHIP

Where the mark is transferred to a new owner the law is clearer. If the mark is in use, and the goodwill in the business is not transferred together with the mark, the new owner must apply to the Registrar for directions within six months, and must then advertise the change of ownership in the way the Registrar directs. When he has done this (but not until then), the transfer of the trade mark will be valid so far as this country goes (although it is not clear whether the transfer then has retrospective effect back to the date when it was actually made); and if the mark was valid before the transfer it will almost (but not quite) certainly be valid in this country afterwards. If there is any doubt whether enough goodwill has been transferred with the mark to satisfy the old rules, it will always be safer to ask for the Registrar's direction: if he does not demand any advertisements, so much the better. An unregistered trade mark used in the same business as a registered mark may be transferred together with it, and subject to the same rules. Otherwise, unregistered marks may only be transferred under the stricter rules of the older law.

If a mark has been registered in the wrong name (for instance, in the name of a shareholder or a director of the company that uses it), a transfer of this sort into the right name will almost certainly be a valid transfer. Whether the registration as a whole is valid will then depend on whether the mark can be attacked as having been wrongly registered in the first place. If the only thing wrong with the registration was the owner's name, the position will then be as follows. If the mark was in use when it was registered, it may have been misleading at the time of registration; it will in that case be vulnerable, although the court will probably refuse to strike it off the register once it is no longer misleading. If the mark was not in use when it was registered, it will now be valid. Such transfers are unpopular with the Registrar, who prefers to avoid all legal technicalities by demanding a fresh application to register in the new name followed by cancellation of the old registration. This course, however, involves a loss in seniority that should not be accepted if a transfer will make the registration valid.

SPLIT OWNERSHIP

Transfers that will result in the ownership of a mark, or of similar marks that are too much alike, being split among two or more proprietors are still not allowed. If there is doubt as to the legitimacy of a transfer, the Registrar may be asked to certify that it is valid; his certificate, if the facts are put to him fairly, will settle the matter once and for all. (But the mark may still become invalid if in fact the public is confused by the two new owners.) Transfers that give one owner the use of the mark for export and another the use of it in this country are valid so far as our law is concerned; transfers that give the mark to different owners for different parts of the United Kingdom are not legitimate unless specially approved by the Registrar. A mark can be transferred for some only of the goods it is registered for, but a transfer leaving goods " of the same description " in separately owned registrations counts as a " splitting " transfer.

The transfers referred to in the last paragraph have to be entered on the register promptly; other transfers apparently need never be registered at all, but there are technicalities which make it important in practice that they should be.

Apart from these rules about splitting, a mark that has not been used can now be transferred quite freely, so far

Trade Marks and Unfair Competition

as this country is concerned. No reference to the Registrar is necessary, except afterwards for the purpose of registering the new owner.

Parallel Imports

There is inevitably conflict between the right of the owner of a trade mark to decide how and by whom his mark shall be used in any given area, and the ideal of free flow of goods that is fundamental to the European Common Market. By and large, Common Market principles prevail. If the owner of the mark has allowed marked goods to be sold in one EEC country, he is not permitted to prevent their resale in the others. Even though the marks in the two countries are in different ownership, if they had a common origin—the two owners were once associated concerns, for instance—movement within the EEC from one to the other has to be allowed (*Centrafarm* v. *Winthrop* (1974)). An agreement between the two owners, to keep out of each other's preserves, will probably be invalid as tending to restrict competition and free flow of goods, even if there is no other connection at all between them (*Sirdar's Agreement* (1975)).

The exact extent to which national trade mark rights can be enforced within the EEC has still to be clearly defined. It seems however that the owner of a trade mark in one EEC country, say Germany, can only prevent imports coming in under the same mark from another part of the EEC if one of the following conditions is fulfilled:

(1) the goods were wrongfully put on the market in the State from which they are being exported; or

(2) the goods were legitimately marketed in that other country but without the consent of the owner of the mark in Germany, and there is not and never has been any "legal, financial, technical or economic link" between the trade mark owners in the two countries.

It has been made clear that these limitations on trade mark enforcement apply only to imports from one EEC country to another, and that trade mark rights still have full force against imports from outside the EEC (*E.M.I.* v. *C.B.S.* (1976)).

Licensing of Trade Marks

The law is uncertain

In these days, a good deal of licensing of trade marks goes on; that is, the owner lets other people use his mark,

Pitfalls in Trade-Mark Law

more or less under his control, and may take payment for the privilege. Before 1938, this sort of thing invalidated any registration; since 1938, it is allowable to some extent, but we still do not quite know to what extent. What the 1938 Act actually says, is that in certain circumstances a trader may be registered as a " user " of someone else's mark, and that use of the mark by a registered user counts in law as use by the owner. That is probably the safer way to go about things. But the tendency of recent decisions is to say that so long as the arrangement could have been the subject of a registration of a user, it does not matter that the registration was never secured.

Registration of users

What the Act provides is that where a user registration is wanted, both parties—owner and user—must apply to the Registrar and show him the arrangement between them. He has a wide discretion whether to register the user or not, but he normally will, so long as the agreement gives the owner some sort of continuing control over the way the mark will be used, so that there is at least the possibility of its remaining under a single control. (It has never been decided, whether the mark becomes invalid if no control is ever exercised; nor whether it matters to what extent the public appreciate what is going on.) In particular, the Registrar recognises as adequate three sorts of control: that of a holding company over its subsidiaries; that given by a contract entitling the owner of the mark to control the quality, etc., of the goods; and that of a patentee over licensees of his patent. In the first case, the marks do not have to be registered in the name of the holding company (although things are tidier that way); in the second and third cases the control can be distinctly unreal.

Licensing of marks used for export

Registered users are not recognised by all foreign countries. In any case, registration of a user in this country cannot of itself give the user rights in countries abroad. If, therefore, both the owner and a user, or two users (registered or not), export goods to the same foreign country, proper arrangements, complying with local rules, ought to be made there; otherwise, the mark may become invalid there. This point needs watching, but the difficulty can usually be overcome; for instance, by passing all the exports of the group through a single company, and transferring to that company the right to use all marks for export together with the whole goodwill in the group's export business.

Marks that are the Name of the Article

Some registered trade marks are habitually used by the general public as the name of the article or substance they are chiefly used on. Typical examples are " Thermos "; " Vaseline "; " Yale " lock; " Hoover "; and " Biro." Such a habit of the public is of great commercial value to the owners of the marks in this class, but from the legal point of view it raises serious difficulties. On the one hand, no mark can be registered for any goods it describes, for if it is descriptive it cannot be distinctive; at the same time, however, a valid registration cannot become invalid simply because the mark is treated by the general public as describing the goods it is used on. Thus, " Shredded Wheat " was removed from the register, because at the time when it was registered it was simply the description of the breakfast food sold under that trade mark (*Shredded Wheat Co.* v. *Kellogg* (1949)) while on the other hand, the registered trade mark " Thermos " cannot become invalid simply because the general public may call any vacuum-flask a " thermos." (This is another advantage of registering marks correctly as soon as it is decided to use them.) If, however, there is a " well-known and established use " of the trade mark, as the name or description of an article, not just by the public but by people trading in the article concerned, the registration will be invalid (unless the use of the mark is confined to the goods of the owner of that mark). Further, such a use in relation to " goods of the same description " is enough to invalidate the mark. Thus, the mark " Daiquiri Rum " had been registered for rum since 1922, but it was removed from the register upon proof that (to persons in the trade) a particular type of cocktail which contained rum, was known as a " Daiquiri cocktail " (" *Daiquiri Rum* " T.M. (1969)).

An ingenious and malicious dealer, by using this rule, could with a little patience and at some risk of an infringement action being brought against him invalidate almost any trade mark that consists of words. In the case of a mark that is already used by the general public as the name of an article or substance, the job of " breaking " the mark should be quite easy. This is not a serious risk (dealers are not normally malicious, though a rival manufacturer might be);

but carelessness on the part of the owners of such marks is. The owners of marks of this type need to keep a careful watch on the language used by members of the trade (on trade journals and dictionaries, especially) to see that careless use of the registered words does not become a habit. Education of the public as well, by suitable choice of advertising methods, to consider the trade mark as a brand name only, will reduce the risk of invalidity. Since, however, it is use by traders that matters from the legal point of view, not use by the public, the state of affairs to be aimed at is one where the trade treat the mark quite strictly as a brand name only while the general public think of it as the name of the article concerned and always ask for that article under the trade mark. In this way legal security can be combined with profitable exploitation of the mark. But an extremely careful watch on the trade will then be essential. Even a most scrupulous trader may fail to appreciate that expressions like " Yale type " are improper.

There are special rules limiting trade mark registrations for the names of chemical compounds and the names of articles for which there were patents that have recently run out. It has been held, too, that the official names of varieties of rose cannot be trade marks.

Non-Use

(a) Removal of disused marks

If a trade mark is left unused for five years it can be expunged, unless its owner is in a position to show that at some time during those five years he would have used it if he had not been prevented from doing so by " special circumstances in the trade." The " special circumstances " must affect the trade as a whole, not merely the particular company that owns the marks.

The five years that matter are up to one month before the legal proceedings start; this gives time for the parties to negotiate, if they hurry, without prejudicing the legal position.

" Use " can be by advertisements, *e.g.* in preparation for bringing out a new line; or it may be on samples imported from overseas; any sort of use " in the course of trade " will do; possibly even advertisements saying " You cannot buy ' — ' because there isn't any." But in that sort of case there are probably " special circumstances " explaining why there isn't any.

Where one owner has two marks, which are too alike to be both registrable if they belonged to different owners and are consequently registered as "associated marks," the tribunal may (and if the one mark contains the other must) accept use of one as a defence to proceedings based on non-use of the other.

(b) Limitation to goods actually used

Where a mark has been used during the past five years for some only of the goods covered by the registration, there can be an application to limit the registration by excluding goods on which the mark has not been used. So where a company had registered marks containing the word "Columbia" for a large variety of goods including both gramophone records and films, and had used it for gramophone records but not for films, the court cut down the registration to exclude films (*Columbia Gramophone Co.'s T.M.* (1932)). The cutting-down was done at the request of a company which wanted itself to use a "Columbia" mark on cinema films. So far as sound-films were concerned, the court accepted the fact that sound-films had not been invented as a "special circumstance" justifying failure to use the trade mark on them.

It follows that a registration that is noticeably wider than the description of goods on which the mark is actually in use may be of limited value in a dispute, though it will often serve to prevent disputes by warning off competitors who might otherwise be inclined to select new marks uncomfortably close to the old one. Strictly speaking, the way to prevent other firms from using a mark on goods not of the same description as those the original owner uses it on is to obtain one of the "defensive registrations" discussed in the last chapter; for defensively registered marks are not meant to be used by their owners and so cannot become invalid because no use takes place. Where a mark is an "invented word" and also is so well known that it undoubtedly can be defensively registered, this may be the best way; where there is doubt whether an application for defensive registration would succeed, it is probably better to keep the "ordinary" registration as wide as possible and hope it will not be challenged.

The Need for Vigilance

If the owner of a registered trade mark allows a mark like it to be used by the trade as a whole it will probably become descriptive or misleading and so invalid; if he allows a competitor to use such a mark, he will seriously endanger his rights. The sequence of events may be as follows: Suppose that A is the owner of a trade mark for certain goods in Class 34 ("Tobacco, raw or manufactured; smokers' articles; matches"). Suppose he has used his mark on pipe tobacco only, and that this particular brand of tobacco is hardly sold outside Devon and Cornwall. Suppose B now starts using a similar mark on cigarettes in a different part of the country—Lancashire, say. B's mark will at first be unregistrable: it will be too close to A's: cigarettes and pipe tobacco are goods "of the same description"; it has already been assumed that the two marks are alike, and it follows that the new mark cannot be accepted by the Registrar while the old one remains registered. In a few years' time, however, B can come to the Registrar claiming that special circumstances now justify registration. If he succeeds in showing that over a considerable area of the country the mark is now distinctive of his goods and not A's, not only may he be allowed to register his mark (at least for cigarettes sold in Lancashire), but further, once his right to registration has been acknowledged by the Registrar, he can demand that A's registration should be cut down to exclude cigarettes. In due course B, if his cigarettes have a wide sale and he is not stopped, may capture the mark entirely.

Such cases illustrate the danger (insisted on in Chap. 9) of too narrow registration of a trade mark. For if A has registered his mark for "pipe tobacco" only, he will be unable to stop B from using a similar mark on cigarettes, so long as no passing-off occurs—and in the example suggested there would be little chance of this. If, on the other hand, his registration covers all forms of tobacco, he will be entitled to stop B at the start; for B will infringe his registration, and infringement will continue until B's own mark is registered. But A must use his rights; he must look out for encroachments on his trade mark and put a stop to them as soon as possible. If he is not sufficiently vigilant, he may find that those rights have ceased to exist.

Foreign Marks

The basic principle of our trade mark law is that the right to registration of a trade mark depends entirely on distinctiveness in this country. There is, in principle, no such thing as ownership of an unregistered mark except the

Trade Marks and Unfair Competition

sort of ownership that comes from having a goodwill in the mark. This leaves our law in some difficulty, in cases where a British trader registers a mark that belongs to somebody else abroad. Quite apart from the problem of "parallel imports," discussed above, our courts seem fairly determined to stop any deliberate appropriation of other people's marks even where they have no sort of reputation here; but there is no real agreement as to how this is to be done. In at least one case, the court has said that a trader who knows that the mark he seeks to register belongs to some foreign firm cannot (as the Act requires of an applicant for registration) "claim to be the proprietor" of the mark. In another case, a trader made a practice of registering as trade marks for toys and the like the names of characters in American television series that might someday reach this country: if the character appeared on British television, he then exploited the mark. The court said that he did not really mean to use the marks at the time of the applications, and so the marks ought to be struck off. Neither answer seems satisfactory in law.

The "Electrix" Story

To end this chapter on pitfalls, here is a cautionary tale; the reader may draw the moral for himself. In 1928, or thereabouts, the owners of the trade mark "Electrolux" (for vacuum cleaners and the like) decided to protect their mark by registering "Electrux"; but they did not use "Electrux." In about 1936, another manufacturer started selling vacuum cleaners under the mark "Electrix." The war interfered, but by 1947 both "Electrolux" and "Electrix" were in use on a large scale; "Electrux" was still not being used. The owners of "Electrolux," provoked (it would seem) by a model called "Electrix-de-luxe," decided that "Electrix" must be stopped. Since, however, "Electrux," which was the mark they would have mainly to rely on, had never been used, it was no good suing for infringement since "Electrux" would merely have been struck off. So they had to set to to use that mark (hurriedly, and quietly lest the "Electrix" people notice the use and apply to strike the mark off before the month was up). So they named a new model the "Electrux." Unfortunately, this model proved unsatisfactory and had to be withdrawn, and conditions being what they were in 1947, it was some time before use could begin again. By the time that "Electrux" could be said to be firmly in use, sales of

"Electrix" cleaners had grown still more. What with this and the years that had elapsed since "Electrix" first came into use, it is not surprising that the court seems to have felt some sympathy with "Electrix"; when in due course an action for infringement was started, the court held "Electrix" to be an infringement of "Electrux," but refused to grant an injunction stopping the use of "Electrix" then and there: this was clearly a case where "Electrix" should be allowed first to go away and try to register their mark. If they got registration (and they had nearly 20 years' use to rely on, by that time, some of it on a very large scale), they would have a statutory defence to the action for infringement and that would be that. So the defendants went away and tried to get "Electrix" registered. Everyone agreed, that the length and scale of their use were amply sufficient to justify registration, so far as any objection based on similarity to the mark "Electrux" was concerned. Unfortunately, however "Electrix" sounds the same as "electrics" which means that where electrical goods are concerned it is one of the totally unregistrable marks.

The cases are *Electrolux* v. *Electrix Ltd.* (1953) (the infringement action, in the Court of Appeal, where it stopped); *Electrix Ltd.'s Application* (1959) (in the House of Lords, the application to register "Electrix").

12

CERTIFICATION TRADE MARKS

The Nature of Certification Trade Marks

This chapter is concerned with a special sort of trade mark intended not to indicate the existence of a trade connection between its owner and the goods it is used on, but to indicate that its owner has certified the goods as reaching certain standards.

These " certification trade marks," as they are called, only superficially resemble ordinary trade marks. They are not really private property at all. Their owners (who are not allowed to be people trading in the goods concerned) must allow them to be used by any trader whose goods reach the required standards; anyone who is denied the right to use such a mark may appeal to the Registrar. Strictly speaking, this right of appeal will only exist if the " Regulations " for the mark say so; but they are unlikely to be approved if they do not. In the same way, it will be an infringement of a certification mark to apply it to sub-standard goods whether the owner has given permission or not. Before the mark can be registered a set of regulations governing the way the mark is to be used and the standards the marked goods are to comply with, must be approved by the Department of Trade. So long as the mark remains registered the regulations can be inspected at the Patent Office.

The standards may relate to " origin, material, mode of manufacture, quality, accuracy, or other characteristic "— *i.e.* any sort of standard will do provided the Department of Trade can be persuaded to take it seriously. A typical certification mark is that for " hand-woven Harris tweed "; less typical, perhaps, are the " kite marks " of the British Standards Institution.

Application

The procedure for registering a certification mark is much the same as for ordinary marks, except that the Registrar cannot accept the application unless the Department of Trade is satisfied that the applicant is competent to certify the goods concerned, that the regulations are satisfactory, and that registration will be to the public advantage. Oppositions to registration by other people can be two-fold:

Certification of Trade Marks

oppositions heard by the Registrar, on the ordinary grounds mentioned in Chapter 10, and oppositions heard by the Department of Trade, on the ground that the Department ought not to have allowed the Registrar to accept the application. In the same way, after the mark has been registered, its validity may be attacked before a court of the Registrar as if it were an ordinary trade mark, or the Department may be asked to cancel it either on the ground that its existence is no longer to the public advantage or on the ground that the proprietor is no longer competent to certify the goods concerned or has failed to comply with the regulations. The Department can also be asked to alter the regulations. It is not unknown, for instance, for regulations to be framed so as to confine use of the mark to the owner's friends. Outsiders might then well object.

In practice the certification trade mark system works without many disputes: the only reported case is " *Stilton* " *T.M.* (1967) where the court, on appeal from the Registrar, allowed the mark " Stilton " to be registered for cheese manufactured by members of the Stilton Cheese Makers' Association, whose rules provided that membership was open to any cheese manufacturer in the counties of Leicester, Derby or Nottingham who agreed to manufacture " Stilton " cheese in accordance with the Association's special recipe.

Infringement

Certification marks are registered in Part A only. They must be distinctive in the same way as other " Part A " marks, and will normally include an indication that they are certification marks. Infringers can be sued in the same way as infringers of any other " Part A " mark; the rules deciding what will be an infringement and what will not are much the same. It is unlikely, however, that the Registrar or the Department of Trade would allow a certification mark to be registered except for the actual goods it is to be used on. and there is no provision for defensive registration, so that the right to sue infringers will usually be somewhat limited. Any use of such a mark on the wrong goods, however, would be likely to be an offence under the Trade Descriptions Act 1968; this is discussed in Chapter 15.

Other Features of the System

Certification marks cannot change ownership without the permission of the Department of Trade, but there are no

Trade Marks and Unfair Competition

other restrictions on changes of ownership. In practice, owners will usually be trade associations or other non-profit-making bodies. The regulations can provide for the owner's own officers to inspect the goods and apply the mark to them; but this is unusual. The usual arrangement is for manufacturers to be authorised to apply the mark to their own goods, under proper control by the owner of the mark. The authorised users of the mark are not registered as users on the Register of Trade Marks; instead, the owners of the mark keep their own register.

A certification mark cannot be removed by the court or the Registrar for non-use (indeed, the court has very little authority over certification marks at all) but the Department would probably be ready in most cases to order unused marks to be taken off the register.

13

THE LAW OF PASSING-OFF

A General Rule

THE general rule governing passing-off has already been stated: it is, that no trader may so conduct his business so as to lead customers to mistake his goods, or his business, for the goods or business of someone else. The present chapter discusses this rule, its ramifications and some partial exceptions to it.

Varieties of Passing-off

Our law lumps together under the name "passing-off" a considerable variety of activities, ranging from simple cases of dishonest trading—where a garage-owner is asked for a particular brand of oil, or a doctor prescribes a particular manufacturer's drug, and the customer is simply given a different and cheaper brand—to cases that are almost cases of infringement of trade mark. In these days, the simple cases are rare; the trades mentioned are unusual in that customers still expect to get something not in the manufacturer's own package. In most shops, goods pretending to be of national brand but supplied unmarked would be immediately suspect. Such things can happen, of course, even if the goods are properly marked—see *Procea* v. *Evans* (1951); and there are more sophisticated versions now and again, such as the manufacturer who declares, untruthfully, that his is the brand you find advertised on television. There are odd cases, too, that fit no general category; whenever one trader manages to benefit from another's goodwill there is likely to be at least an arguable case of passing-off. By and large, though, cases of passing-off are akin to infringements of trade mark, but are cases that do not quite fit into the scheme of the Trade Marks Act.

"Badges" and Reputations

Most cases of passing-off, then, are cases where a trader without in so many words saying that his goods are someone else's, nevertheless indicates this by applying to his goods some badge or sign that people have come to regard as a mark of that other's goods. In the simplest case, this badge may be an ordinary trade mark—perhaps a trade mark that for one reason or another is not registered for the goods concerned. (If it is so registered, there will be an infringement as well as passing-off.) It may be the name of a business, or of someone associated with the business. It may be a special appearance or "get-up" of the goods: a specially shaped package, for instance, such as a Coca-Cola bottle. But all such cases have these essentials in common: the "badge," whatever it may be, must be one that has come by use in this country to distinguish the goods of a particular trader or group of traders; and it must have been copied, whether deliberately or by accident, closely enough for people to be deceived, or at least to be confused. So the plaintiff in an action to stop the passing-off must prove two things: that the mark or other "badge" he is relying on has a sufficient reputation amongst customers; and that there is a real risk that what the defendant is doing will lead to deception or confusion of those customers.

The risk of deception

Judging the risk of confusion in these cases is not unlike judging whether one of two trade marks infringes another (a matter we have already discussed). But in a passing-off action the question is not whether any fair use of the defendant's mark or other "badge" would be likely to cause confusion, but whether what the defendant is actually doing is fair or unfair, so that a court may have to look at all the circumstances to see whether they increase or decrease the risk. It may be important, for instance, whether and how the defendant puts his own name on his goods, and what if anything his name will mean to the customer. It may also be important to what extent the customers already know where the goods come from. A business dealing direct with manufacturers probably knows very well whom it is buying from, and is unlikely to be confused by misleading markings; it is when the goods get into shops that misleading markings really matter.

"Get-up"

It will be clear from what we have just said, that cases of passing-off by "get-up" are not very common. Very few manufacturers these days put the real emphasis of their advertising upon the mere look of their package. Even if packages did not change as often as they do, it would still be more sensible to put the real emphasis on a brand name. So the public are taught to look for the name, and they do; and are not deceived by similar packages with a different brand name or none at all. There was a case a few years back (*White, Hudson* v. *Asian* (1965)) where the court held that merely to use an orange-coloured wrapper for wrapping cough-sweets was passing-off; but it happened in Singapore, where many customers could not read the names printed in European lettering on the rival wrappers. The evidence was that the plaintiff's sweets were there known and asked for simply by words meaning " red paper cough sweets."

Business names

Many passing-off actions are concerned with business names, just because these cannot be registered as trade marks are. (There is a register of business names, and registration is compulsory in many cases, but it gives no right to stop others using the name. The companies registry has power to object to company names that are deceptive, but it accepts differences far too small to provide a defence to a passing-off action.) Actions about business names are much like actions about trade marks: the plaintiff has to show on the one hand that people have come to associate the name in dispute with him, on the other that the defendant's version of it is misleadingly similar to his. In judging similarity, it is particularly important what sort of customers are concerned, and this may depend on whether and in what form the name goes on to the defendant's goods. If the defendant's name is merely used as a company name, in dealings with other companies and so on, it may remain unknown to anyone not capable of telling the two businesses apart. Once it gets on to the goods the general public may see it and be confused by it.

Exceptional cases

In certain special cases, the law accepts as inevitable a certain amount of confusion, and the court will not interfere so long as the defendant does nothing dishonest and nothing to make matters worse.

Use of a man's own name

People have a right to use their own name in business, even though they have a surname that is better known in the trade concerned as the name or trade mark of someone else. But a man who takes unfair advantage of the possession of such a name will be restrained from doing so; and the books record far more cases where the courts have interfered with the use men were making of their own names than cases where the court has let them go on. In particular, there is no special right to form a company embodying one's name, except in the special case of an already established business becoming a company and merely adding " Limited " to its old name. (An established company may claim a right to trade under its name very much as an individual may; but if a new company is formed with a name that is confusingly similar to that of some other business, the court will usually order it to change that name.) Nor is there any special right to trade under one's surname alone; nor any special right to mark one's name on goods, where the general public may see it and be misled by it. Readers needing further warning of the dangers of assuming a right to trade under one's own name may care to look at *Wright's* case (1949) and the *Parker-Knoll* case (1962).

Descriptive names and marks

Those who choose to carry on business under a name that does little more than describe the business cannot complain if others do the same, and must put up with quite small differences between their trading name and other people's. Thus in a case (1946) between rival office-cleaning companies, it was held that the names " Office Cleaning Services " and " Office Cleaning Association " were not too close. In the same way, those who choose as trade marks words which virtually describe the goods should not complain if others describe their goods in similar terms. But in all these cases, the court will intervene if the defendant is dishonest. A defendant who is trying to get his goods or business mistaken for someone else's will find the court very ready to believe that he has succeeded.

Marks that the public treats as descriptions

Special difficulties arise with those very well-known trade marks that the general public treat as merely the name of the article concerned. If a man goes into an ironmonger's shop and asks for a new Yale lock, he may be wanting one made by the Yale people themselves, but he may just mean that he wants an ordinary pin-tumbler cylinder lock without caring whom it is made by. There may be genuine confusion between him and the shop assistant as to which is meant; or a dishonest shopman may use the ambiguity as an excuse. As one of the *Aertex* cases (1953) illustrates, this may make it very hard for the owner of such a mark to prevent its misuse.

It may be noted that the courts have held that, on the one hand, where a former trade mark had become descriptive adding the word " Genuine " to it did not make it into a trade mark again (" Genuine Staunton " for Staunton-pattern chessmen: *Jacques* v. *" Chess "* (1940)) whilst on the other, use of someone else's trade mark is not made permissible by adding the word " type." A Scottish judge has indeed described the word " genuine " as almost as sinister in significance as the word " type " (" *Harris Tweed* " case (1964)).

Geography and the wine cases

It may be as misleading to say, untruly, that goods come from a particular area (as with " Scotch whisky ") as to use the wrong trade mark on them. In such cases, any trader who has a legitimate claim to use the place name concerned for his goods may sue the trader who misuses it for passing-off (" *Spanish Champagne* " case (1960)). But place names, and especially anglicised place names, may become merely descriptive of things made in a particular fashion. And there may be intermediate cases in which the meaning of a geographical term may depend on context. Thus it has been held that " Champagne " necessarily connotes wine (of a particular sort) from the Champagne district of France, and that its use for similar wine made in Spain cannot be justified even if it is expressly labelled " Spanish champagne." " Sherry " is to some extent ambiguous: used alone, it connotes wine (of a particular sort) from the Xeres region of Spain, but such expressions as " South African sherry " are legitimate (" *Sherry* " case (1967)). " Burgundy," on the other hand, may in this country mean really nothing at all, so that only the fastidious confine its use to wine that actually comes from Burgundy.

ODD AND UNUSUAL INSTANCES

Where the plaintiff does not trade

There can be passing-off even though there is no trade or business in the ordinary sense concerned; thus the professional institutions can (and now and again, have to) sue both people who put letters after their names so as falsely to pretend to a professional qualification, and people who form societies with similar initials so as to give members something they can put after their names. There have been passing-off actions about *noms-de-plume* as well as about the titles to books and plays. But there has to be some sort of business connection, in a wide sense, between the plaintiff and the sort of thing the defendant is doing, so that the court can be satisfied that there is a real likelihood of the plaintiff's suffering damage to some sort of business interest if the defendant goes on with what he is doing.

In recent years there have been a number of cases concerning merchandising rights in popular characters. They arise in the following way: a manufacturing organisation takes a well-known television or radio personality—real, fictional or even mythical—and exploits the popularity of the character in the advertising and selling of his goods. The question arises: can the character concerned (or in the case of fictional and mythical characters, their creators) take action to prevent such exploitation? Again, the answer turns on whether there is any business connection or "common field of activity" between the plaintiff and the defendant. Thus, it was held that a well-known broadcaster could not sue to prevent the giving to a breakfast food of the name he used on radio ("*Uncle Mac*" case (1947)), whilst in interlocutory proceedings the courts have refused to restrain a builders' skip hire business from using the name of mythical television creatures (*Wombles* v. *Wombles Skips* (1975)). In another case (*Tavener Rutledge* v. *Trexapalm*, "*Kojak*" case (1975)), a lollipop manufacturer, who had taken a franchise to use the name of a television character associated with lollipops, found himself enjoined from using the name (pending a full trial) at the suit of a rival manufacturer who had built up a reputation selling lollipops under the name without taking a licence.

Authors and artists have special protection from the Copyright Act 1956, against attribution to them of works that are not theirs or works of theirs that have been altered.

Other odd instances

The ordinary case of passing-off concerns the sale of goods in such a way that purchasers will be deceived or confused as to whose goods they are. But there can be passing-off where the goods come from the right manufacturer: by selling secondhand goods as new, or spoilt goods as sound, or lower-priced goods as superior ones. There can be passing-off where sellers are confused as to

The Law of Passing-Off

the identity of the buyer instead of the other way round. There can be passing-off where the defendant's name cannot be objected to and it is his address that is confusing. A single case will illustrate these last two possibilities (*Pullman v. Pullman* (1919)). The defendant, a former director of the family firm, many years later set up on his own, under his own name (as he was entitled to do). Then he altered the name of his house to resemble that of one of the plaintiffs' factories (in itself, probably legitimate: it is not passing-off to call a private house by a name confusingly similar to that of someone else, so long as no business is involved). But he then moved his business office to his house and wrote from that address to people who had been supplying the plaintiffs with materials, offering to buy from them. That was held to be passing-off.

SUING FOR PASSING-OFF

Most ordinary actions for passing-off follow one of two patterns. One is, that the plaintiff acts at once, on learning of the passing-off. He starts the action and at once applies to the court for an interlocutory injunction to stop the passing-off temporarily, until the case can be brought to trial. It takes about a month for the parties to prepare written evidence from a few important witnesses and bring the case in front of a judge, who decides on the spot whether the case justifies a temporary injunction or not. By that time, both parties know enough of the strength of the other side's case to have quite a good idea of how the trial is likely to turn out, so there is no point in actually fighting the action any further.

The other pattern goes like this. The plaintiff waits for months, or even years, before taking any action. It is of course too late to ask the court for an interlocutory injunction; it is the plaintiff's own fault that the case was not tried long ago. There is no way the parties can accurately assess each other's cases, or see how the matter looks to a judge, without taking the dispute to trial. At the trial, the plaintiffs must prove at length, by evidence from those concerned with the trade, how well known their business or their goods are and how confusing whatever the defendant is doing is. The defendant for his part produces witnesses who have never heard of the plaintiffs; witnesses who by that time have got used to the two parties having similar names or similar trade marks (or whatever the dispute is about); witnesses who are too alert to be confused

Trade Marks and Unfair Competition

by any state of affairs worth arguing over at all. The trial will be long and expensive, because of the large number of witnesses. The outcome will be uncertain, because of the difficulty of knowing how the evidence will turn out and what the judge will think of the witnesses. Furthermore, by the time the case comes to trial the trade and public generally have got used to having these two businesses or trade marks about and have learnt to distinguish them; so that what was passing-off when it started may have ceased to cause serious confusion by the time the case comes to trial.

The moral is left to the reader.

14

SLANDER OF GOODS

THE GENERAL RULE

THIS chapter deals with a different sort of unfair competition, known variously as trade libel, slander of goods, slander of title, or injurious falsehood. It consists of injuring someone else's business, by making, from some "indirect or dishonest motive," a false statement to some third person. Real financial loss (or the real risk of it) must be shown by the plaintiff.

The law on this matter is best seen by considering a few examples.

EXAMPLES

De Beers v. *General Electric* (1975)

The plaintiffs and the defendants were both manufacturers of abrasives made from diamonds. The defendants had circulated to prospective customers a pamphlet purporting to show by the results of scientific tests that the plaintiffs' products were inferior to those of the defendants. On an application by the defendants to strike the action out as disclosing no reasonable cause of action, it was held that when "puffing" of goods turns to denigration of the goods of a rival, there comes a point where this becomes actionable, and that if a reasonable man might consider that an untrue claim was being made seriously, and with malice, then the plaintiff disclosed a reasonable cause of action.

Greers v. *Pearman & Corder* (1922)

The defendants had a registered trade mark. It included the words "Banquet Brand," but the register included a disclaimer of any exclusive right to the use of those words. The plaintiffs, who were manufacturers in the same trade, used the word "Banquet" as a name for one of their lines. The defendants' solicitor (for whose actions the defendants were responsible) wrote to the plaintiffs' customers claiming that this was an infringement of the registered trade mark, and thereby spoilt the sales of the line concerned. The judge told the jury that if the letters were written in the honest belief that there was an infringement they must give a verdict for the defendants; but if the letters were not written honestly they must find for the plaintiffs. The solicitor, as well as the defendant company's secretary, knew that the entry in the Trade Mark Register included the disclaimer, and the jury found for the plaintiffs.

Hayward & Co. v. Hayward & Sons (1887)

The defendants, having brought a passing-off action against the plaintiffs and lost, issued advertisements that made it look as if they had won. The plaintiffs brought another action, successfully, to get these advertisements stopped.

Mentmore v. Fomento (1955)

The defendants had sued a third party for infringement of patent and had won; but there was an appeal from the decision to the House of Lords still on foot. The plaintiffs were (or so at least the defendants thought) infringing the same patent. The defendants approached a large store handling the plaintiffs' goods, just at a critical moment from the point of view of the Christmas trade, and indicated to the buyer that if the plaintiffs' goods were not withdrawn from sale at once the defendants would get an injunction against the store. The defendants knew very well that, until the appeal had been decided, they would get no injunction against other infringers. The court granted an injunction to stop the defendants telling people about their successful patent action without disclosing the full facts.

Riding v. Smith (1876)

The false statements concerned need not relate directly to the business. This was a case where the plaintiff's trade decreased, because of rumours that his wife, who served in his shop, had committed adultery. It was held that this was good ground for an action.

CONCLUSION

Enough examples have been given to show the scope of this sort of action. It must not be assumed that such actions would always be won by the plaintiffs; traders are apt to say that other people's goods are worse than theirs, and even where such statements are demonstrably false a judge will not necessarily decide that they are dishonest. There is this further difficulty (*cf.* what was said at the end of the previous chapter, about suing for passing-off) that interlocutory injunctions are very rarely granted in these cases, if the defendant intends to try at the trial to show that what he said was true. Litigation is always uncertain, however, and it is wisest not to do anything that can result in an action reaching a court. The safe rule is never to make disparaging statements about a rival business or its products.

15

THE CRIMINAL LAW

INTRODUCTION

THERE are a variety of Acts of Parliament dealing with methods of trading which are so objectionable as to be made criminal. Most of these Acts are concerned with particular types of goods or trading (for example, the Food and Drugs Act 1955, or the Trading Stamps Act 1964) and it is outside the scope of this book to discuss them. But the Trade Descriptions Acts 1968–72 are of general application.

THE TRADE DESCRIPTIONS ACTS 1968–72

It is a criminal offence under the Acts to apply a " false trade description " to any goods, or to supply (or offer to supply) any goods to which such a " false trade description " has been applied. The words " trade description " are defined almost as widely as one can possibly imagine. They consist of " an indication, direct or indirect, and by whatever means given, of any of the following matters with respect to any goods or parts of goods, that is to say—(a) quantity, size or gauge; (b) method of manufacture, production, processing or re-conditioning; (c) composition; (d) fitness for purpose, strength, performance, behaviour or accuracy; (e) any [other] physical characteristics; (f) testing by any person and results thereof; (g) approval by any person or conformity with a type approved by any person; (h) place or date of manufacture, production, processing or reconditioning; (i) person by whom manufactured, produced, processed or reconditioned; (j) other history, including previous ownership or use."

A " trade description " can be applied to goods in almost any manner, including orally or in advertisements. No offence is committed unless the " trade description " is false. This ordinarily means that the public must be likely to be misled by the trade description into purchasing the goods. Thus in *Kingston Corporation* v. *F. W. Woolworth* (1968), decided under the old law, the court held that the description " Rolled Gold " applied to a pair of cuff-links sold by the defendants for 4s. was not an offence even though only the fronts of the cuff-links were coated with a thin layer of poor quality gold. On the other hand, if the trade description is completely false, it probably does not matter if the public will be misled or not. Thus in *Kat* v. *Diment* (1950), the expression " non-brewed vinegar," when applied to something which was not in fact vinegar, constituted an offence even though there was no indication that the public would be misled.

The Acts have similar provisions dealing with descriptions of services and accommodation. Thus false descriptions of holidays and holiday accommodation have been well kept down by the Acts after a number of successful prosecutions. The Acts also attempt to deal with unfair price tags (such as " 3p off " tags on articles which in fact were never sold for the higher price). The 1972 amendment deals with the application of misleading indications of British origin to imported goods.

The practical working of the Acts

(i) *As an alternative to civil action*

Though the scope of the Acts is vast, civil proceedings by a trader affected by their breach are almost always preferable if, as is generally the case, there is also a civil wrong. This is for a number of reasons: firstly the civil court has power to grant an injunction to restrain further acts of the type complained of and, in many cases, an injunction can be obtained very quickly; secondly the award of costs in a civil court is much higher than in a magistrates' court; thirdly the procedure in a civil court is, generally speaking, much easier than in a magistrates' court; fourthly the magistrates' court has no power to award damages or an account of profits; finally the result even of a successful prosecution is unlikely to be more than the imposition of a small fine (£400 is the maximum).

It follows that in practice the Acts have had their main application not in the field of protecting traders against unfair competition but rather in the field of the protection of the public at large—" consumer protection."

(ii) *Enforcement provisions*

Unlike earlier Acts upon the same subject, the Trade Descriptions Acts make someone responsible for their enforcement. It is the duty of local weights and measures authorities (who employ inspectors) to take proceedings under the Acts, and they are empowered to make test

Trade Marks and Unfair Competition

purchases, enter premises (subject to certain conditions), and seize goods for the purpose of ascertaining whether an offence has been committed. To a certain extent the local inspectors are subject to control by the Board of Trade, which can, for instance, prevent multiple prosecutions.

At the moment action is only taken on simple, plain cases where the public is in need of protection quickly, and it would appear that in most cases inspectors only act if they receive a number of complaints from the public. There is certainly nothing to prevent anyone who feels injured by another's passing-off or infringement of trade mark from reporting the matter to a local inspector: this will generally produce some result, if only a warning letter to the culprit.

The Acts do not give a trader who suffers particular injury by a breach of their provisions any civil remedy as such, although there may also be a corresponding civil wrong, e.g. passing-off.

(iii) *Trade marks and the Acts*

It might be thought that if the Registrar of Trade Marks were prepared to let a trade mark be registered its use by the owner upon goods within the registration would not be an offence under the criminal law. This is not so. Therefore, whenever a trader is considering a new mark for one of his products he should not only choose a mark which is registrable, but also one which will not cause him any trouble with the criminal law. It would be best for him to ensure that in use his mark could not, even remotely, be said to be a " false trade description." (This is yet another reason why totally meaningless words often make the best trade marks.)

For those traders who already had a trade mark registered or used when the 1968 Act came into force on May 30, 1968, there is a limited immunity; they do not commit an offence if they were not committing an offence under the old law. The exception is of limited value, for, if use of the mark is an offence now, there probably was an offence under the old law although nobody bothered about it. Thus if a label were registered for clothing as a whole, and included such words as " all wool " (or even, without containing such words, had become associated in the minds of the public exclusively with wool), it would have been an offence under the old law to use it on non-woollen clothing, just as it is an offence now.

We have already referred to the difficulties which can

The Criminal Law

occur in relation to licensing the use of trade marks (see Chap. 11). Further difficulties may arise under the Trade Descriptions Acts; for example a trade mark used by someone with the permission of the owner may well give "a false indication, direct or indirect . . . of the person by whom goods are manufactured or produced."

Finally in relation to trade marks, we should point out that the use of a certification trade mark either by an unauthorised user or otherwise than in accordance with the rules is an offence, for the wide words of the definition of " trade description " (in particular items (g) and (b)) are clearly enough to cover such cases.

Conclusion

Although the Acts are drafted in such wide terms they are used mainly in flagrant cases: borderline cases and ingenious defendants remain the problems of the civil courts.

PART IV

COPYRIGHT

16

INTRODUCTION TO COPYRIGHT

INTRODUCTION

WE discussed in Chapter 6 the use of copyright law to protect industrial designs; but that is not what the Copyright Acts were meant for. They were meant for the protection of authors, artists and composers and to provide a legal foundation for the innumerable transactions by which authors, artists and composers are paid for their work. This chapter is concerned with the wider field of copyrights.

THE NATURE OF COPYRIGHT

The primary function of copyright law is to protect from annexation by other people the fruits of a man's work, labour, skill or taste. This protection is given by making it unlawful, as an " infringement of copyright," to reproduce or copy any " literary, dramatic, musical or artistic work " without the consent of the owner of the copyright in that work. It is works that are protected and not ideas; if ideas can be taken without copying a " work," the copyright owner cannot interfere. This distinction is a difficult one to draw, both theoretically and practically; it is discussed in some detail in Chapter 19. Here is an example. If a photograph is taken of a landscape, that photograph will be copyright: good or bad, it counts as an " artistic work." It will be an infringement of copyright (subject to exceptions dealt with in Chap. 20) if, without consent, that photograph is reproduced—either in the sense in which a newspaper would " reproduce " it by making blocks from it and using them for printing, or in the sense in which it could be said to be copied, if an artist were to sit down with the photograph in front of him and make a painting out of it. But it would not be an infringement for another photographer to take a similar photograph of the same land-

Introduction to Copyright

scape: the landscape is not copyright, for the photographer did not make it (the position might be different if he had), and the second photograph, though using the idea of the first, would not be a reproduction of it.

COPYRIGHT, REPUTATIONS AND COMPETITION

Nor is it the function of copyright to protect personal or business reputations, or to prevent business or professional competition: it can sometimes be useful for such purposes, but these uses are in a sense accidental. Thus it is no infringement of copyright to imitate an author's literary style, or to take the title of one of his books, or to write a book about characters he has invented—though any of these things may be unlawful for other reasons, if people are misled into thinking that he is responsible for the imitation. Thus also it is normally no infringement of copyright to copy another firm's brand name or one of their advertising slogans. (Here again such acts are likely to be unlawful for reasons discussed elsewhere in this book.) It may or may not be an infringement of copyright to use a photograph of a respectable actress to adorn the cover of a disreputable magazine: it depends who owns the copyright in that photograph. The actress's remedy for that sort of thing is an action for libel.

On the other hand, if in such a case the actress does happen to own the copyright in her photograph, an action for infringement of copyright is likely to provide the quickest and cheapest way of dealing with the matter. So also, though an advertising slogan will probably not have copyright, a complete advertising brochure is likely to be copyright as a " literary work," while any photograph or drawing in it is likely to be copyright as an " artistic work." Such works may be trivial from an artistic or literary point of view, but they have to be very trivial before they lose protection altogether, and commercially they may have great value. A trade mark may consist of a picture—like the "His Master's Voice" dog—or of one of the "house logos" so fashionable nowadays, and the copyright in the picture or logo might be of great value in supplementing ordinary trade mark protection. A fake painting may well be built up largely of bits painted from genuine ones; if it is, and the genuine ones are not so old that their copyright has expired, the fake will infringe and a copyright action may offer the best way of dealing with it.

Copyright

Types of Copyright Dispute

Copyright disputes (other than disputes about industrial designs) tend consequently to fall into three groups. There are the rare straightforward cases where a substantial work has been pirated for its own sake. There are also many cases where the original work has little intrinsic value or has not been reproduced in any ordinary sense, and where copyright is invoked for ulterior reasons, usually of a commercial character. In between come those cases where the work copied is a substantial one embodying a great deal of skill or labour—a directory or a time-table or something of that sort perhaps—but nevertheless its value derives more from such things as goodwill than from the labour put into it. In cases in these last two groups there is apt to be a lot of argument as to whether copyright law applies to the case at all.

Copyright in Practice

Although reported copyright disputes tend to fall mainly into these last two groups, the practical and commercial importance of the copyright system lies elsewhere. The main function of the copyright system is to provide a legal foundation for transactions in " rights ": to provide a legal sanction behind the customary arrangements by which, for instance, a composer is remunerated when some of his music is used on radio or in a film. It is very rare for such matters to give rise to litigation, and very rare for ordinary people to be concerned with them or to find out much about them. But many of the provisions of the Copyright Act are framed as they are so as to fit into this system; there are some oddities in the Act as a result, partly because the standard forms used in the entertainments industry are traditional rather than reasonable and American rather than English.

Copyright and Confidence

It is not the function of copyright to prevent betrayal of confidence, whether personal or commercial. But the conditions under which English law protects confidences as such are somewhat limited (they are discussed in Chap. 22), and copyright may be a valuable additional weapon. For instance, an ordinary business letter may be indiscreet without being confidential, and may fall into the hands of competitors without any illegality that will allow the courts to intervene.

But even a business letter is a "literary work" and so copyright. There may be no way to stop a competitor into whose hands it falls from showing it to customers, but he can be stopped from making copies of it for circulation.

OLD COPYRIGHTS

As will be seen in Chapter 17, copyright lasts a very long time. The present Copyright Act was passed in 1956, and came into force on June 1, 1957. There are still many works in existence that have copyright although they were created before the present Act (or even its predecessor) came into force, and to some extent it is necessary in dealing with them to refer to the old law. For most purposes, the position is, that if such works are copyright at all they are governed by the present law; they may, however, have lost copyright (or never have had it) although by present-day reckoning they are still new enough to have a copyright still in force. Such cases are not of sufficient practical importance to justify detailed discussion of the old law in a book such as the present one: it is usually sufficient to assume that the 1956 Act was retrospective in its operation. In dealing with pre-1957 works, however, this point should never be entirely forgotten.

"REPRODUCTION"

It has already been pointed out that the word "reproduce" as used in copyright law has rather different meanings in different contexts. This difficulty runs right through our copyright law. If we speak of one book being copied from another, this is not the same sort of "copying" as occurs when (for example) a painting is made into a plate to illustrate a book. In fact the "copyright" in a work of literature and the "copyright" in a painting are not really quite the same sort of thing: the "copyright" in a song is again something rather different. Nor is the legal protection needed by the author, or by the publisher of a novel, really the same as that needed by the author of a song (who is mainly concerned to stop its being sung or recorded without payment) or by an architect (who is mainly concerned to ensure that anyone wanting a house such as he would design will employ him as architect and not a competitor). A sculptor on the other hand will get his main protection from the general law of property, and his copyright is unlikely to be of great value. The Act does differentiate between

Copyright

different categories of "works," as we shall see, but for many purposes it lumps them all together.

The word "reproduction" is, however, not used in copyright law in the sense in which music is often said to be "reproduced" by a wireless or a record player. That, in copyright language is "performance by means of a mechanical instrument" and not "reproduction," and different rules apply to it. The Copyright Act in fact speaks of "reproduction in a material form": it is the record itself (or the printed score) that is the "reproduction."

17

WORKS THE SUBJECT OF COPYRIGHT

"Works"

COPYRIGHT extends to almost everything, published or unpublished, that can be called "a work" at all—at least if it was produced in this country. The Copyright Act mentions as among the subjects of copyright: novels and other "literary works"; tables and compilations, which count as "literary works"; lectures, addresses, speeches and sermons; plays, scripts for cinema films, ballets and "entertainments in dumb show," all of which count as "dramatic works" (the film itself is a work, but of a different category); paintings, drawings, engravings, photographs and similar things (such as photo-lithographs), sculpture, works of "artistic craftsmanship" not covered by any other head, and works of architecture—all counting as "artistic works"; music; gramophone records, tapes, perforated rolls and other devices for reproducing sounds; sound and television broadcasts; and the typography of books. It is of some importance to which category a work belongs since—see Chapter 20—the rights of the copyright owner depend on it. A detailed list of "works" in which copyright can exist is contained in the Note to Chapter 19.

Foreign "works"

Foreign works are protected if they come from a country (or a citizen or inhabitant of a country) with which we have made a treaty to that effect; China is almost the only one which does not qualify (Russia and E. European countries do). The foreign countries concerned likewise protect British works more or less as they protect local ones. But some countries (the U.S.A. in particular) require copies of the work to be marked © with the name of the copyright owner and the year of first publication. This is often forgotten on commercial publications, and sometimes forgotten on books.

Merit, originality, and various sorts of works

In general, works are protected regardless of merit. Thus a rather ordinary tie-on business label has been given protection as an "artistic work" (*Walker* v. *British Picker*

Copyright

(1961)), as have drawings of simple machine parts (*British Northrop* v. *Texteam* (1974), referred to in Chap. 6). They must be "original," in the sense of not being entirely copies of another similar work—in other words they must "originate" from their authors. They must also be substantial enough to deserve the name of "works," though here again (as the case just mentioned shows) the standard is not high. A ballet need not be good, but must be reduced to writing. But a play is not deprived of copyright because it is a bad play, or a painting because the artist is completely lacking in skill or taste.

Artistic craftsmanship

The term "work of artistic craftsmanship" is not quite clear. In the leading case on the subject (*Hensher* v. *Restawile* (1975)) the members of the House of Lords expressed differing views on its interpretation, but were unaminous in holding that ephemeral, nailed-up prototypes of a three-piece suite were not works of artistic craftsmanship. The expression would include hand-decorated pottery, but a court has hesitated to say that it includes a dress. There has to be something "artistic" as well as an element of "craftsmanship." This can be important when it comes to industrial designs. When a machine part is made from drawings, there will be copyright in the drawing; but when it is made by a craftsman simply playing with a bit of metal until he gets it right, there is at present no copyright unless either the thing can be classed as "sculpture" or there is something artistic about it. Pure craftsmanship will not do; nor will the modern sort of designing, where a computer expresses itself directly in metal without making a drawing first. It has, however, been proposed that copyright protection should extend to works which start their life in three dimensions, whether or not they could be described as works of sculpture or "works of artistic craftsmanship." It has also been proposed that computer programmes which have involved sufficient skill and/or labour should be given clear and effective copyright protection, which protection would extend to works produced with the aid of a computer. The author of such a work would be the person who devised the computer's instructions.

Photographs and sound-recordings

Photographs and sound-recordings are not restricted as to merit or subject-matter, but like any other works they cannot be copyright unless they are "original," and this needs some consideration. In a sense, no photograph or sound-recording is original: for the camera or microphone only records what is presented to it. But there is more to making a photograph and much more to making a sound-recording than that, and the skill of the photographer or recording engineer will found copyright just as will the skill of the artist who makes an engraving from a painting. It is the change of form of the work that in these cases justifies copyright. Where there is no change of form, copyright must be justified in some other way; a mere re-photographing of a photographic print, for instance, would not give the second photograph a copyright of its own. For this there would have to be sufficient alteration combined with the re-photographing to make the second a different "work." But it may be assumed that in any practical case, whoever did the re-photographing could show that enough additional skill and originality was put into it to give the new photograph a new copyright. So in the field of sound-recording, whilst a "mere" re-recording (as distinct from conversion of a "monophonic" recording into "stereo," or something like that) would give no additional copyright, in practical cases, such as transfer from old 78 r.p.m. records to long-playing, it should be assumed that the recording company has done enough to make a new copyright. This is much the same problem as that of a new edition of a book: see below.

Triviality

In copyright disputes of a commercial character, the main issue in the case is often whether that which has been copied embodies enough "work, labour, skill or taste" to be called an original work. It is not easy to lay down any clear rules as to this, for it is essentially a matter of opinion —of the opinion, that is to say, of whatever court tries the dispute. The opinions of judges are never very easy to forecast, for they necessarily depend a great deal on the precise circumstances of the case in which the issue concerned arises. For instance, few judges can avoid giving some weight to their opinion of the relative merits and morals of the parties to the dispute, and not all judges try. Nevertheless, it is possible to give some idea of the probability that a particular "work" will be held to have copyright.

Copyright

Different authors

The first question that arises, is how much of the " work " derives from any particular author: for it is only the part for which he is responsible that can be considered in deciding whether he has produced an original work. Suppose for instance that a textbook has run, as legal textbooks often do, into a large number of editions in the course of a great many years. The first edition was no doubt copyright; perhaps it still is, perhaps that copyright has lapsed. Each subsequent edition may or may not give rise to a new copyright in the whole book, depending on whether the amount of work done by the editor in producing the new edition is sufficient to be called the creation of a new work. (It does not matter for this purpose whether the new edition is edited by the original author or by someone else; the test is the same in either case.) A similar problem arises in connection with a publication such as a railway time-table, which is reprinted perhaps monthly with a very few alterations from one month to the next. In connection with a textbook this question is usually not very hard to answer, though the answer is hard to put into words; one can " feel " the difference between making minor or routine alterations in the book and making a more substantial contribution to the book as a whole. In other cases the distinction may be very hard to draw, and when this is the case courts tend to reach illogical decisions that confuse matters still further. It has for instance been held that each successive monthly edition of the Index to a railway time-table had a copyright of its own, although this Index was merely a list of railway-station names, and there were, on the average, only about ten changes made in this list each month. Probably the true moral to be drawn from this particular case, is that if a " work " in fact embodies a great deal of labour, it is unsafe to copy it in reliance upon a purely technical defence to copyright proceedings. For such an Index would clearly have been copyright if it had been produced entirely afresh; the only difficulty arose from its having grown up gradually over a period of many years. It would be a surprising thing, if a work were to be refused copyright merely because it had taken years to produce, and no court would hold this to be the law if it could help it; it is however the law in some cases.

" Anything worth copying is worth protecting "

One way of approaching the problem of where to draw the line between that which amounts to a " work " and that which does not, is to say that anything worth copying is worthy of protection against copying. In many cases this rule is a useful guide. But the line must still be drawn somewhere, and the difficulty of drawing it tends to be most acute just in the sort of case where this rule is not applicable: in those commercial cases where something has been copied, not so much to avoid the trouble of producing something similar, as for extraneous reasons. The most that can be said with certainty is that any sort of drawing may be held to have copyright; that even a few bars of music may have copyright, at any rate if they are recognisable; and that although a single sentence (such as an advertising slogan) has never yet been held to be copyright, anything more may constitute a "literary work." (The title of a book, for example, is not copyright, and protection for it must be sought in an action for passing-off.) Merit is not necessary, but a composition that is striking—"original" in the ordinary as distinct from the copyright sense—is more likely to be protected by the courts than a commonplace composition of the same size or length. Even so, short business letters have been held copyright notwithstanding a characteristic absence of signs of literary skill. So have advertisements in newspapers.

Compilations

It is particularly difficult to lay down rules for determining whether there is copyright in a compilation or arrangement of facts or of non-copyright material. There will clearly be copyright in such things as telephone directories, *Who's Who*, railway time-tables or mathematical tables, if they are "original." Messages sent out by news agencies have been held copyright, even where literary form was not involved—as with stock-exchange prices; so have a week's radio programmes; so have the starting prices for a race (which took some skill in sorting out), but not a list of starting positions (which were merely written down as they were determined by ballot); so has an anthology of poems, not themselves copyright; but not an edition of a non-copyright book shortened by cutting out about half of it. (In the last case, there were critical notes published with the new edition and these were held copyright.) Copyright has been refused to a local time-table, made by selecting and rearranging entries from a larger time-table relating to a particular town, and it has been refused to a selection of seven non-copyright tables of conventional type for inclusion in a diary.

Copyright

About all that can be said in general is that mere industry counts less than knowledge, skill or taste in such matters; that the amount of labour that goes into a particular compilation is of great importance; and that anything published in permanent form—a book, for instance—has a better chance of protection than such ephemeral productions as a notice on a notice board. The rest is a matter of how the court feels about it. In the case of the diary, for instance, the Court of Appeal decided one way, the judge who tried the case at first instance and the House of Lords the other; a sure sign of the sort of case where anything can happen.

An ordinary book of non-fiction may well be copyright on two separate grounds: both from the literary skill that went into writing it and from the skill and labour that went into selecting the facts set out in it. Historical facts for example are not copyright in themselves, but a selection of them can have copyright as a compilation. Here again the line is difficult to draw: a compilation of facts will have copyright, but mere ideas will not. This, however, is a question that belongs to the discussion of " infringement " in Chapter 19.

COPYRIGHT CAN EXIST ONLY IN " WORKS "

It is worth emphasising that apart from questions of amount —of whether there is enough of a product for it to count as a " work " for copyright purposes—nothing can attract copyright unless it is the sort of thing that is called a " work." For instance, it will be an infringement of copyright to film a play without consent, but not to film a dog-show or a boxing match: the one is a " dramatic work," the others are not, for nobody has composed or arranged precisely what happens at them. If the promoters of such spectacles want to prevent photography, they must do it in some such way as by not selling tickets to people who do not agree not to take photographs. So also, a card-index system is not copyright: nor is a game, though the written-out rules of the game will be and so may any board on which it is played. Thus the inventor of a new game may be able to prevent other people copying his board or his book of rules, but if he wants to stop them playing the game, he must seek a patent for it. A collection of five-letter code-words was held copyright as a " literary work " (skill was needed in selecting the words so as to guard against errors in transmission) but not a system for coding the wholesale prices in a catalogue: however ingenious a system, and however successful in concealing the retail profit from customers, it was a mere scheme and not a " work." The instructions for decoding the prices could have been copyright: but that copyright would not be infringed by a competitor who wrote his own instructions, quite independently.

ILLEGAL AND IMMORAL WORKS

By way of exception from the general rules, the courts will not protect a work that is illegal, immoral, indecent or similarly undeserving of protection. A libellous poem for instance cannot claim copyright, nor can an obscene picture. Inevitably, a great deal depends on the attitude of the judge trying the case. Late in 1939 for example, copyright protection was refused to a would-be humorous document entitled " The Last Will and Testament of Adolf Hitler "; while not obscene, it was in the view of the judge vulgar and indecent. Presumably however some people thought it funny, or it would not have been worth publishing, let alone worth copying too. The judge concerned was not one of them but, if he had been, the case would probably have gone the other way. Cases of this sort being rare, the limits of this exception have never been very clearly laid down.

OVERLAPPING COPYRIGHTS

It is in general irrelevant to the question whether a work is copyright, to consider whether it is covered by some other copyright too. In the case for instance of what are called " collective works "—symposiums, magazines, encyclopedias and so on—there must necessarily be a whole series of copyrights in the separate articles or stories as well as a copyright in the work as a whole: in the general plan and arrangement of the work.

Overlapping copyrights are found not only in collective works, however. In Chapter 16, it was pointed out that a painting can be a reproduction of a photograph for copyright purposes. In such a case there will be a copyright in the painting separate from that in the original photograph: the painting is an " artistic work " in its own right, requiring skill and labour for its execution, notwithstanding that the scene depicted is taken from a photograph. In such a case it will be unlawful to reproduce the painting unless the owners of both copyrights consent. Similar cases are common in other arts too: for instance, in a record of music, both the music itself and the recording will be copyright, unless the music is quite old. The point is important

Copyright

in dealings in copyright, for it will be ambiguous to refer to "the copyright in the painting," if more than one copyright exists in the painting, and an agreement using such language may have rather unexpected effects. See Chapter 21.

Translations

A translation will have copyright, independently of the work from which it is translated. The classic example of this was a case where the court had to decide upon the ownership of the copyright, if any, in a book said to have been dictated to a "medium" by the spirit of a biblical character who had died some 2,000 years before. The court noted that the book was written, not in any language current in those days, but in somewhat archaic English, and decided that the translation from one language to the other must have been done by the medium—who consequently had a translator's copyright. The case is *Cummins* v. *Bond* (1926): the full report ([1927] 1 Ch. 167) is well worth reading as itself a "literary work." It must not be supposed that the judge necessarily believed the book to have been dictated by any spirit; but a judge has to decide an ordinary civil case on such evidence as the parties choose to put it before him. Since both parties accepted that the book had a ghostly origin, it was proper for the judge to decide the case on that basis.

It should be noted that the matter translated need not be anything that is capable of sustaining a copyright; the test to be applied is whether the translator has expended a substantial amount of labour, skill and knowledge upon making his translation. If he has, it will be copyright.

Other cases

In the same way, a shorthand report of a speech has its own copyright; here it is the shorthand-writer's skill and labour from which the copyright derives. The speech will in itself probably be copyright too. The photograph of a painting, or painting made from a photograph; the film made from a book or play and the "book of the film"—all are similar instances. In these cases there are two copyrights (at least): one, that in the original work, covers both works; the other covers the transformed work only. So again an architect's plans will be copyright as plans—unless of course they are merely copied from other plans. If a building is built from the plans it will attract architectural copyright which is quite distinct from the copyright in the plans. Finally, there is a copyright in the typographical arrangement of a published edition of a work, which is separate from the copyright in the work itself: see the Note to Chapter 19.

THE PERIOD OF COPYRIGHT

Copyright in ordinary literary, artistic, musical and dramatic works lasts a very long time: during the author's life and for 50 years after (or rather, until the end of the fiftieth year after that in which the author dies—this rounding-off to the end of the year applies to all periods of copyright). Note, however, that the copyright in artistic works used in industrial designs can only be infringed by industrial use for a 15-year period beginning with the date upon which the mass-produced article is first marketed: see Chapter 6. Literary, musical and dramatic works and engravings will have even longer copyright if they are not exploited (published or performed in public or recorded and sold as records) whilst the author is still alive: in that case the 50-year period begins at the end of the year of first exploitation, but it has been proposed that the law relating to unpublished works should be changed to give a maximum copyright period of the author's life plus 50 years. For photographs, recordings, films and other more special types of work there are shorter periods, listed in the Note to Chapter 19. Exceptionally, works belonging to the Crown have only a 50-year period (but, as before, it mostly begins with the year of first exploitation); and there are similar provisions for works that are genuinely anonymous or pseudonymous—in the sense that the author's identity never really becomes known. If a work has joint authors, the period is taken from the life of whichever dies last. (A work consisting, say, of words and music by different people is not a joint work in this sense: the copyright in the words and that in the music may consequently expire at different times.) Most books nowadays carry the year of first publication, and gramophone records now have to; but in general it is not easy to find out when copyright expires.

18

THE OWNERSHIP OF COPYRIGHT

INTRODUCTION

IN considering ownership, it should be remembered that in this country, copyright comes into existence automatically (if at all), without need for formalities. The result is that it is possible for the question of ownership never to arise at all, until the copyright is the subject of some dispute. It will then be necessary to work out who is the owner, with no assistance from registers or formal documents. The rules of law governing ownership are therefore important: fortunately, they are simple too.

This chapter deals with the question of who owns a copyright in the first place; what may happen to it afterwards is a different question altogether and will be considered in Chapter 21.

THE BASIC RULE—COPYRIGHT BELONGS TO THE AUTHOR

Apart from the exceptional cases mentioned below, copyright belongs in the first place to the author of the work concerned. The author, for this purpose, is the person who actually expends the work, labour, knowledge, skill or taste by virtue of which the work is copyright. In the case of a book for instance, the "author" of the letterpress will be whoever composes the sentences of which it is made up. If a man dictates a book to a secretary, he will be the author —not his secretary; if on the other hand he merely provides the ideas, and the secretary writes the book, the secretary is the author—whether the book is published in his name or not. (But the employer probably gets the copyright—see exception (ii) below.) If a book is illustrated by drawings, the "author" of the drawings will be whoever drew them, notwithstanding that the idea for each illustration was taken from the book itself. There may of course be books where, although one man wrote the whole text, another provided and selected the material for the book and determined its arrangement to a sufficient extent to be considered a joint author of it. In general however the man who chooses the actual words used will be the sole author: for instance, where a "ghost" writer composes a man's autobiography for him, the " ghost " will be held to be the sole author even though the subject of the autobiography supplies such facts as may be included. It has even been held that the compiler of a work such as *Who's Who* is the " author " of each of the entries, although the material for the entry is supplied by the person concerned in response to a questionnaire.

In the case of a photograph, the " author " is not the person who takes the photograph but the person who owns the film at the time when the photograph is taken. It is, however, proposed that the author should be the person responsible for the composition of the photograph. In the case of a sound-recording the " author " is the person who owns the original record at the time when it is made.

Exception (i)—Commissioned works of certain types

Where the work is an engraving, photograph or portrait, or a sound-recording, and is commissioned by someone who pays or agrees to pay for it, and there is no agreement to the contrary, the copyright belongs to the person who gives the commission. In the usual case, which is the case of a photograph which is also a portrait and is made to the order of the sitter, the question is: what happens if the sitter does not want any prints from the portrait? Does he have to pay for prints whether he wants them or not or for the sitting if he takes no prints? If so, and if nothing is agreed to the contrary, the copyright will be his. But if the sitting is free, and there is no obligation to take prints, the photographer will have the copyright; for he will be the owner of the negative and so he is the " author." Note that ownership of the negative does not go with the copyright: the photographer will almost certainly own the negative whoever has the copyright, and will be entitled to hold on to it. The point is, that ownership of the copyright does not in this case (as it usually does) go with ownership of the negative. Thus if the sitter gets the copyright, he cannot have access to the negative to make more prints without coming to an arrangement with the photographer; nor is the photographer entitled to make prints from the negative, for any purpose, without the consent of the sitter as owner of the copyright.

As an example of a borderline case, consider a photograph taken at a wedding, or a school prize-giving, to which the photographer was specially asked to come, but without payment—the intention being, that he should make his profit from selling prints of his photographs, and it being reasonably certain that enough prints would be ordered

Copyright

to make the job well worth getting. Who gets the copyright? Probably the photographs were "commissioned," but whether there was an agreement to pay is a more difficult question: a court held under the previous Act that the school authorities who arranged for the particular photographs concerned got the copyright in them, but on slightly different facts the decision might well have gone the other way, and the language of the present Act is different. So is the attitude of people like judges to people like photographers.

It is not of great importance in these cases who started the negotiations which resulted in the "work" being made: a photograph may be "commissioned" although the photographer asks for the commission, and a portrait may be painted on the sitter's suggestion without being "commissioned." In the latter case the painter will get the copyright in the first place even though the sitter may later buy the finished portrait from him, and as we shall see in Chapter 21, the copyright does not necessarily pass to a purchaser of the picture.

It seems to be sometimes forgotten that this rule as to "commissioning" works is confined to photographs, portraits, engravings and sound-recordings. It does not apply for instance to architectural works. A man who gets an architect to design a building for him pays for the plans and gets them; but he does not get the copyright either in the plans themselves (as plans) or in the building itself, unless he makes a special arrangement to that effect. The copyright belongs to the architect as "author"—or in the case of the plans, more probably, as the author's employer: see the next exception. This means not only that the architect may copy the plans before handing them over, and make use of the copies next time he has a similar building to design—it also means that the building owner has no right to reproduce his plans or his building beyond erecting the building or buildings envisaged by his contract with the architect (for which there will be an implied licence in the contract), although he may "reconstruct" the original building from time to time. If the building is a factory or store, for instance, he cannot repeat the design of the original building in a similar building in another town, without the architect's consent; while if the building is a house on a housing estate, he needs the architect's consent before using the same design on another estate. The simplest way of getting this consent is of course to employ the same architect again.

The Ownership of Copyright

It has been proposed that the law relating to commissioned works should be changed, so as to vest the copyright in all cases in the author (or his employer), subject to an exclusive licence to the person commissioning the work for all purposes reasonably within the contemplation of the parties at the moment of commissioning. The proposals would also give the commissioner the power to restrain any exploitation of the work for other purposes against which he could reasonably take objection.

Exception (ii)—Works by employees

When the author of a work is in the employment of some other person " under a contract of service or apprenticeship," and the work is made " in the course of his employment," the copyright belongs to the employer. (By way of exception, if the author's job is to produce material for a newspaper or magazine, the author keeps the copyright, unless his contract says otherwise, except so far as publication in newspapers and magazines is concerned.) This does not include cases where the author can be loosely said to be " employed to produce the work," but is not employed in the ordinary sense—in effect, it means somebody whose National Insurance stamps are partly paid for by an employer. Thus the editor or publisher who commissions a book or article gets the copyright only if the author's contract says so; the publisher who hires an author (by a " contract of service ") gets the copyright automatically, just as if the man were hired to make boots—there would be no need for a contract saying that the boots would belong to the owner of the factory. In the same way, the architect who is " employed " to design a house does not lose the copyright in his design to the building owner; but the architect's draughtsman, who works for a salary, will be an employee, and the copyright in the plans he is paid to draw will belong to the architect who employs him. The exact limits of the phrase " in the course of his employment " are not very easy to define: it is said that this phrase has given rise to more litigation than any other in the English language. For most purposes however it means simply: that it was part of his job to produce that work. One example is the architectural draughtsman already mentioned. On the other side of the line, there was a case where a translation had been made by a man for his employers, but in his spare time and for extra payment (as distinct from an overtime payment). It was held that the translator, not his employer, was the first owner of the copyright in the translation. (It may be, the employer could have demanded that the copyright be handed over to him; but this question did not arise, for it was not his employer that the translator was suing.)

The proposals for the reform of copyright law would retain the exception in the case of works by employees, subject to this: that if a work produced by an employee in the course of employment is exploited (either by the employer of by someone else with the approval of the employer) in a way which was not within the contemplation of the employer and employee at the time when the work was made, the employee should have a statutory right to an award from his employer. With the introduction of such a provision, the exception in favour of journalists, mentioned above, would be abolished.

Crown Copyright

The Crown has much wider rights than a private employer. Where a work is either prepared or published, by or under the direction or control of a government department, the copyright belongs to the Crown—unless there is an agreement with the author to the contrary. The Crown does not always enforce its copyrights—it allows such things as Acts of Parliament to be freely reproduced from the official editions published by the Stationery Office; but the copyright is there, and it is enforced in relation even to such apparently public works as Ordnance Survey maps, or directions from Ministries to local authorities. As was stated in the last chapter, copyright in these cases lasts for 50 years from publication; a provision which has the merit that it is possible to find out whether the copyright in Crown works has expired without having first to find out who the author was: an almost impossible task in the case of, say, an Ordnance Survey map. It has been proposed that the special provisions in relation to Crown copyright should be brought to an end, so that the Crown would be in the same position in relation to copyright as any other employer, or a person who commissions a work.

Where Authorship is not Certain

If a work appears to be signed, or to bear an author's name, the courts will assume unless it is proved otherwise that the man whose name or signature the work bears is the owner

The Ownership of Copyright

of the copyright in it; if not, the first publisher will be presumed to own the copyright. These are however merely rules of evidence; they do not alter rights, but sometimes make it easier for the plaintiff in a copyright action to prove his case. In particular, they make it possible to sue for infringement of the copyright in an anonymous work without disclosing the author's name.

19

WHAT IS INFRINGEMENT?

INTRODUCTION

It was pointed out in Chapter 16 that copyright is in essence merely a right to stop other people doing certain things (the "acts restricted by copyright"). The definition of infringement is consequently of very great importance. The present chapter sets out to explain, just what are these activities that an owner of a copyright is entitled to stop; the rules stated in this chapter are however subject to certain exceptions discussed in the chapter following.

INFRINGEMENT BY REPRODUCTION

First of all, copyright in a work will be infringed if the work is copied without the consent of the owner of the copyright. To give a simple example, consider an article in a magazine. In the ordinary way of course, it will have been sent in by the author (or by his literary agent); sending it in will mean that he owns the copyright and he wants it published so long as he gets the proper fee—and the only possibility of argument lies in the size of the fee. It is only when something goes wrong that a dispute about copyright can arise. Suppose he sends in illustrations with his manuscript and they are not his to offer for publication; then each copy of the magazine "reproduces" them without the consent of the copyright owner, and that is infringement. (The man who sent the article in pays the damages, if he has the money.) Or the whole article may be very like one that appeared earlier in some other magazine, but not quite the same. This may or may not constitute an infringement of the copyright in the earlier story according to circumstances; and it is necessary to consider in some detail, just where the line is to be drawn.

Copying

Although the Copyright Act does not use the word "copy" in this connection (it speaks of reproducing the work concerned, or a substantial part of it, in a material form), copying is essential to this sort of infringement. It has been said often enough that six monkeys, operating

What is Infringement?

typewriters at random, would sooner or later reproduce all the books in the British Museum Library; among them, works that were copyright. But there would be no infringement of the copyright, for there would be no copying: the work would have been reproduced quite accidentally, without reference to the original. We suggest, as a couple of exercises for the reader, two problems. First, would a novel thus created by the monkeys be copyright, and if so, who would own the copyright? Secondly, if someone goes through the output of the monkeys—or of a computer printing at random—until he finds the complete text of a popular novel (as he must, sooner or later), is publishing that an infringement?

Copying need not be direct, and it need not be conscious or deliberate. All that is necessary for an infringement (so long as a substantial part of the earlier work is taken), is that the later work should somehow, through some channels, be derived from the earlier. On the other hand, this amount of copying is necessary, and must be proved: for if the copyright owner wishes to stop an infringement, he must prove to the appropriate court that infringement has taken place.

Proof of copying

The difficulty of proof is often a serious one. It will very seldom be possible to prove directly that copying has taken place: for only the alleged infringer himself knows how his work came into existence. The result is that in practice the only thing to do is to point to the resemblances between the two works and to say that these resemblances are too many and too close to be due to coincidence; the court can then be asked to infer that some sort of copying must have taken place. If the court accepts this argument it will then be up to the alleged infringer to explain the resemblances away if he can. That is to say, he must produce a reasonable explanation of how those resemblances could have come into existence without any copying. Not every explanation will do, for judges are not exactly credulous people; if the explanation is that Mr. X thought the whole thing up himself, without ever having seen or heard of the earlier work, the judge will want to see Mr. X (or hear some good reason why he cannot see Mr. X) and find out whether to believe the story or not. But if the explanation is reasonable, the copyright owner must find some other way of proving his case, and as we have said, there is usually no

Copyright

other way available. An interesting case on this point is *Francis Day & Hunter* v. *Bron* (1963) where the court held that although there were very great similarities between the plaintiffs' tune "In a Little Spanish Town" and the defendants' "pop" song "Why," this was not enough to prove infringement where the composer of "Why" (whose story was believed) said he could not remember ever hearing the plaintiffs' tune although he was prepared to admit that he might have heard it on the radio when he was young.

A substantial part must be copied

When it has been shown that copying has taken place, the next requirement for proving infringement is to show that the part of the one work reproduced in the other is a substantial part. The question: what is a substantial part of a work? is very similar to one discussed in Chapter 17: what is substantial enough to be called a work?

(a) Where a part is copied exactly

Here the principle that what is worth copying is worth protecting can be given full scope. Once a court is satisfied that there is a copyright work, and that the defendant in the case before it has thought it worth while copying out word for word some part of that work, it will be very hard to persuade that court that the part copied was not substantial. Thus where four lines of a short poem of Kipling were reproduced in an advertisement, the court found no difficulty in holding that this was a substantial enough part of the poem for there to be infringement. As usual however a lot depends on how the court feels about the case. Where for instance the title of a short story was taken from the refrain of a popular song, and four lines from the song were printed below the title (as of course quotations often are), the court held that this was not an infringement of the copyright in the song. The line must be drawn somewhere; the owner of the copyright in the song was not really deprived of his property or of an opportunity to draw profits from his property; and regarded as a literary work, the song was not quite in the same class as a poem of Kipling.

This question of merit is rather a difficult one. Strictly speaking, it is not easy to see how the merit of a work should affect the matter at all. In practice, it is always easier to found a successful action for infringement of copyright upon a work that has merit than upon a work that has not. The law is never absolutely rigid, and the court will give a common sense decision where it can. It is fortunate that this is so; but it is sometimes in consequence a little difficult to forecast what the court's decision will be in any particular case. The imponderable influence of merit (or the lack of it) in copyright actions is one of the things that make forecasting difficult.

A very instructive case as to what is a substantial part of a work arose from the inclusion, in a newsreel of a military parade, of a sequence taken while the band was playing the copyright march "Colonel Bogey." The sequence lasted less than a minute, and other things were happening at the same time, but the principal air of the march was clearly recognisable. This was held to amount to taking a substantial part of the march; the more so, because the sound-track of the film could have been used by itself as a record of the march—to provide incidental music during an interval for instance. There is now a special provision excluding infringement in cases where music is merely picked up by the microphone of a newsreel camera, and not specially recorded to provide a background to the film.

(b) Compilations

The simplest examples of compilations are of course works like directories, consisting of a large number of short entries without any particular literary form. Here the rule as to infringement is clear. It is a "reproduction," and so an infringement, to take the entries from one directory for use in another, even if they are independently checked against some other source of material and then completely rearranged in combination with other material. It is legitimate, however, after compiling a directory from other sources, to check it against a rival work to see that there are no mistakes or omissions. It is not so clear to what extent entries that are found to have been omitted from the new compilation may at this stage be copied into it from the old: a few may be, a substantial number may not, but exactly how many may be depends upon the circumstances of the case. In particular, it depends a great deal on whether the judge who tries the case really believes that the second work was independently compiled before the checking took place. Compare *Peacey* v. *De Vries* (1921), where the court believed it, with *Blacklock* v. *Pearson* (1915), where the court obviously did not.

Copyright

The same rule as for directories has been applied to a translation of a foreign play, and is probably applicable to any work considered as a collection of information. That is to say, where a work has copyright by reason of the skill and labour that went to collecting the information given in it, that copyright will not be infringed by using the work as one source among others, to supplement and correct information obtained in the main elsewhere. That copyright will, however, be infringed, if any substantial part of the information set out by the work is taken as a whole, even if it is afterwards cross-checked against other sources. This is, of course, not the only test of infringement: for most works will also have copyright by reason of their literary or artistic form, and this latter copyright will be infringed if the form is taken whether the information set out is taken or not. To this question of reproduction of form we must now turn.

(c) Where there is merely a similarity of form

In discussing this question, it must first of all be remembered that there is no copyright in ideas. Thus an illustrated joke, for instance, will have copyright as a picture, and possibly even the words of the caption might be copyright: but the joke itself cannot be. There will consequently be no infringement if the same joke is used by someone else, differently phrased and with a different picture. In the same way it is no infringement of copyright to take the plot of a book, even in fair detail. In one case, for instance, there was issued with a set of gramophone records of operatic music a fairly full synopsis of the action of the opera: this was held not to be an infringement of the libretto of the opera. Nor would the position be in any way different if that synopsis had been written up into a complete new libretto for a similar opera: for there would have been nothing common to the two works except the synopsis, and this did not infringe any copyright.

It must also be remembered that every competent worker in any field must be expected to be familiar with any important work that has gone before; and it is just the important and successful work, that everyone ought to know and that will inevitably influence works that come after it, that is likely to attract infringers. In fiction it is indeed often the poor and unknown author whose unexpectedly brilliant work is stolen from him, but in real life that sort of thing seems not to be a commercial proposition.

What is Infringement?

The inevitable influence of one work on those that follow it does not involve infringement of copyright. The difficulty is to distinguish between drawing on the common stock of experience, and making improper use of other people's work.

Judges have tried to express the way the line is to be drawn, by saying that for there to be infringement, one work must produce the same effect as the other. To put it slightly differently, there must be something that might make people encountering the two works in succession feel, " I have read this story—or seen this play—or heard this music—before." An example may help to explain how such tests work out in practice.

Many years ago, one Austin composed a new arrangement of the music of a work that had long ago lost any copyright it had ever possessed: the " Beggar's Opera." The new arrangement was of course copyright; it was also a popular success. A manufacturer of gramophone records, wishing to take advantage of Austin's success, brought out a recording of extracts from the " Beggar's Opera." Since the tunes were all old, this was not in itself any infringement of Austin's copyright. But the recording went further: although the actual notes were not copied from the Austin arrangement, the tunes were " dressed up in the same way," as the judge put it. That was infringement: a record is a " reproduction." The case in fact raised in a different context the same question as the example discussed in Chapter 16, of the photographer who sees a successful photograph of a landscape and goes and takes another like it. He may photograph the same view, for there is no more copyright in a view than there was in the tunes of the " Beggar's Opera." But he must not go further and imitate to any substantial extent the tricks by which the first photographer has converted the view into a successful photograph.

The Austin case illustrates also the way in which the circumstances of a case influence the court's findings. The defendants there had advertised their records in a way that emphasised the relation with Austin's successful arrangement, and in fact in this connection lay the whole reason for bringing out those records at that time at all. This made it by no means easy for the defendants to argue that they had really taken nothing from Austin: the defence was in effect merely that, as a technical legal matter, what they had done was not reproduction of a substantial part of that which was the subject of copyright. Purely technical defences are always dangerous. If such a question arises on a comparison of two apparently independent works, the case is not prejudiced by any admissions that the one work is connected with the other, and such a defence takes on a rather different aspect. The defendant can, and does, argue that there has been no copying at all in any ordinary sense; that the resemblances between the two works if not pure coincidence—any two works being indeed much more alike than perhaps their authors would admit—are the result of the sort of unconscious influence mentioned above as inevitable and legitimate; and that these resemblances are trivial, not substantial. (He may even argue that the resemblances are due to legitimate " quotation " of phrases that the hearer will be expected to recognise as coming from earlier works). Only then does he argue that in any case, what is common to the two works is not the sort of thing that the law calls " reproduction." If there is real doubt as to the copying, the technical defence will have a much more favourable reception.

(d) Changes in material form

A rather similar sort of question can arise where there is a change in the material form taken by a work; for instance, to take examples that have come before the courts, where it is suggested that a dress infringes a drawing of a dress, or a shop-front an architect's sketch of a shop-front. Clearly the two cannot be identical, in either case, but there is still a sense in which it can be said that there can be reproduction of one work by the other. Whether there is reproduction or not in any particular case is a question on which opinions are likely to differ, with the result that it is likely to be very hard to forecast what view the judge who decides the case will take. In this particular case, of a three-dimensional " reproduction " of a two-dimensional work, it is specially provided that nothing shall count as a reproduction unless recognisable as such by people not expert in the subject-matter concerned, although it has been proposed that this particular provision should be repealed. Just how inexpert a person you have to take is anybody's guess: a High Court judge will probably do, though they are apt to complain about it—see Chapter 6.

OTHER FORMS OF INFRINGEMENT

In the case of " ordinary " literary, dramatic, musical and artistic works, reproduction (in a material form) is the primary form of infringement. For more special works there are special rules, and for "ordinary" works there are other sorts of infringement. These things are listed at the end of this chapter, and only instances will be mentioned here.

Adaptations of literary or dramatic works

It is an infringement of the copyright in a literary or dramatic work to make or reproduce an "adaptation" of it. Adaptation includes translation, and conversion into a strip-cartoon, as well as conversion of a literary into a dramatic work and vice versa. Cases about conversions and other adaptations are often very difficult, for they raise in acute form the same sort of difficulty as has already been discussed in connection with the phrase "reproduction of a substantial part of a work." Such a conversion need involve no detailed copying: a novel could be converted into a silent film, for instance (which would be "reproduction" of a dramatic adaptation, if not "reproduction" of the original work) without taking a single word—there would indeed be no words apart from occasional captions. This would be an infringement, if done without consent. If instead a sound-film were produced, it could still be an infringement, notwithstanding that the dialogue was independently written without any copying from the novel. In the same way, it has been held in one case that a ballet infringed the copyright in a short story; there could be no question of using the same words, but the ballet nevertheless "told the same story." Simply taking the bare plot does not constitute infringement in such a case; the incidents of the story must be taken too. But it is not necessary for the two works to resemble one another to the extent needed for one novel to fringe the copyright in another novel, or one play in another play. A most instructive discussion of the question of infringement of the copyright in a play by a silent film may be found in *Vane* v. *Famous Players* (1928). We know of no case that lays down any principle as to how to decide whether a play infringes the copyright in an artistic work such as a picture; perhaps the court would look for an actual reproduction of the picture upon the stage.

Films

It may be noted that where the making of a film infringes copyright, infringement has probably already taken

Copyright

place before actual photographing begins: the reproduction of, or conversion into a dramatic work of, the work whose copyright is infringed, will already have happened in the preparation of the script from which the actual film is made. The actual making of the film will be a further infringement by the making of a "contrivance" for performing the work. In the same way, there was a case where a maker of gramophone records had a right to record a song but no other rights in it. He wanted the recording to be made with orchestral accompaniment, which the published version lacked; so he had a single manuscript copy prepared of the song with a suitable accompaniment. The preparation of this manuscript was held to be an infringement of copyright: arrangement or transcription of a musical work is "adaptation" and so infringement.

Publishing unpublished works

If a work is unpublished, it will be a separate act of infringement to publish it (in the sense of issuing copies of the work to the public) without consent. This sort of infringement very seldom occurs alone, for publication is impossible unless copies of the work are in existence and the production of the necessary copies will normally itself constitute infringement. It may be important, however, for large damages may flow from it: in particular, the author's own chance of successful publication may be completely spoilt by an anticipation.

Performing a work in public

It is an infringement of copyright to perform a work in public without consent. (The same applies to public performance of anything close enough to a work, for its reproduction to infringe copyright). "In public" has here a rather special meaning. It refers, not to the sort of place where the performance takes place, but to the sort of audience that is present. Nor does it mean that the performance is one that anyone can attend who likes, still less that a charge must be made for admission. For this purpose, any performance is "in public" that is not restricted to members of the home circle of whoever is responsible for the performance. Guests can be present of course; there can be a very large party to see or hear the performance: but it must be a genuinely domestic affair or it will be public for copyright purposes. An amateur dramatic show by members of a Women's Institute for

What is Infringement?

fellow members only; "Music While You Work" in a factory; music played so that it could be heard in the public parts of a restaurant—all these have been held to infringe copyright as "performances in public." There is an exception (for the recording copyright only—see the Note below) where a sound-recording is performed without charge as part of the amenities of a place where people sleep or as part of the activities of a non-profit-making club.

"Performance" for this purpose includes performance by means of a mechanical instrument: such as a cinematograph projector, a gramophone or wireless, a television receiver. So that showing a film in public is both "causing the film to be seen in public," involving the film copyright, and a performance in public of any play or music embodied in the film; and similarly with sound recordings. Further, although artistic works cannot be "performed" it is infringement to exhibit them on television.

If a studio performance of a play is "televised" (or a studio performance of music is broadcast), and the broadcast received in the presence of such an audience that it is "in public," this will be a performance in public of the play or music for which whoever operates the receiving set will be responsible: he will infringe unless he obtains the necessary consent. In addition, the broadcaster has a separate copyright in his broadcast: but this copyright is not infringed unless there is a paying audience. Thus public display of a television receiver—a demonstration receiver in an ordinary shop for instance—will give rise to an infringing performance in public if what is televised is a performance of a work; a completely impromptu performance, however, will have no copyright but the broadcaster's copyright, which is not infringed unless the audience pay. Thus the interposition of a wireless link, or of a cinema camera and projector, between a performance and its audience never prevents copyright from being infringed; but it may give additional possibilities of infringement.

There is a similar distinction made for tape-recordings of sound broadcasts. It is an infringement of copyright to record a work, whether by way of tape-recording of a broadcast or otherwise, unless the making of the record is a "fair" dealing with the work for purposes of research or private study; see the next chapter. But the broadcaster's copyright in the broadcast is not infringed by a record of it made for private purposes.

Copyright

Getting others to infringe and like cases

In accordance with ordinary rules of law, it is as much an infringement to get someone else to do an infringing act as to do it oneself. In particular, an employer is responsible for acts of infringement committed by his employees " in the course of their employment." Copyright law goes further, and makes it an infringement to authorise an infringement: for example, an author who offers a manuscript to a publisher to publish authorises the publisher to do so; and if the publisher sends it to a printer he authorises the printer to reproduce it. (It is usual for publishing agreements to make the author warrant to the publisher that the book infringes no copyright; but even without this warranty, the ordinary law would enable the printer to recover from the publisher, and the publisher from the author, any loss they had suffered as a result of copyright trouble.)

" Authorising " covers other things too: any case where someone who does not control a copyright accepts a royalty for its use would be authorising the use, even though the initiative came entirely from the user. With the growth of sophisticated commercial photo-copying techniques, those who make available photo-copying facilities, for example in libraries, should take special care to avoid being taken to authorise the use of those facilities for the purposes of infringement (*Moorhouse* v. *University of New South Wales* (1976)). It should be noticed, however, that merely knowing that someone else is going to infringe copyright is not inducing an infringement: to sell a man a copy of a play, for instance, with a warning that it must not be publicly performed, can never be an infringement unless it is a copy of a pirated edition. What the buyer intends to do with it when he gets it is not the seller's affair. Such a sale without a warning is also probably safe, since a purchaser ought not to assume that he has any right to perform the play: with films the position is different; see Chap. 21.

In one respect, copyright law goes even further than that. It is infringement merely to permit a place of public entertainment to be used for an infringing performance, "permit" meaning merely being able to stop it and not doing so. In this case, however, if the permission was not a source of profit, it is a defence that the giver had no reason to suppose there would be an infringement. The point of this provision is that the actual performers may well not be worth suing.

What is Infringement?

Commercial dealing

Another sort of infringement, and an important one, is commercial dealing in works which infringe copyright. Generally speaking, this covers any sort of commercial dealing (including, for instance, free distribution on any appreciable scale as well as sale); but it is limited to infringing copies. A copy which was lawfully made abroad can however infringe here, making importation and dealing with it unlawful, since the copyrights in different countries are separable. To some extent, the provisions against dealings are limited to dealings by those who know that the copies are infringing copies, but an innocent dealer caught with copies in his hands can usually be made to give them up, and may be liable in damages if he cannot or will not do so.

The position is too complex for detailed discussion here, but an example may serve to illustrate it. The traveller on the Continent, who brings home a book for his own " private and domestic " use, infringes no copyright; but an infringing copy may be seized by the Customs on entry, if the copyright owner has taken the trouble to ask them to. Even though the importation was not an infringement, the book is still treated as belonging to the copyright owner (see Chap. 1) and he can demand its surrender. The importer must then surrender it, and if he cannot (having sold it or thrown it away, perhaps) will be liable in damages unless at the time he genuinely believed, and with reason, that it was an authorised copy.

Architectural works

If this is possibly unduly favourable to the copyright owner, the rules governing architectural works sometimes run the other way. The owner of an architectural copyright cannot stop completion of an infringing building once it has started, and may find it very hard to get evidence of infringement (even if he knows of the infringement) until construction has started—and has got far enough for the form of the building to be apparent. Nor can he insist on being taken in as architect. All he can do, once construction has started, is to sue for damages. Now architects work for modest scale fees, so that a copyright owner who is an architect could not hope to make more than the scale fee out of the building; and most of that is attributable to the work he does for it and not to his ownership of copyright. Thus the amount left, which is all that he can be said to have

Copyright

lost as copyright owner through not being employed on the infringing building, is rather small.

NOTE: "WORKS"

A list of the different sorts of "work" is given below; together with the period of copyright, and the definition of infringement, for each sort. Infringement is defined in terms of the "acts restricted by the copyright" for the sort of work concerned.

It must be remembered that a work may incorporate more than one copyright, and the various copyrights must be considered separately (there is an exception to this, mentioned below, in connection with cinematograph films).

What was said above about dealing with infringing copies applies to all sorts of work; so does what was said about "authorising"; but "permitting a place of public entertainment to be used for an infringing purpose" is infringement only of literary, dramatic or musical copyright.

1. Literary and dramatic works

The period of copyright is 50 years from death of the author or publication, whichever is later, but is has been proposed that the law should be changed, so that the maximum term of copyright in literary, dramatic, musical and artistic works would be 50 years from the death of the author. The acts restricted by the copyright are: reproduction; publication; performance in public; broadcasting; offer for sale of records of the work; adaptation or doing of the above acts to an adaptation.

"Publication," here and below, means issuing copies of the work to the public (*cf.* its meaning in patent law). The sending out of a programme on a diffusion service is (here and below) equivalent to broadcasting. "Adaptation," in relation to these works, means conversion from a non-dramatic to a dramatic work or vice-versa (with or without translation into another language); translation; conversion into a strip cartoon.

There are various exceptions from the definition of infringement mentioned in the next chapter; and one (not there mentioned) for recitations in public by one person of part of a work.

2. Musical works

The period of copyright, and acts restricted by it, are the same as for literary works, except that "adaptation" now means arrangement or transcription of the work. In addition to the exceptions mentioned in the next chapter, there is a provision (see Chap. 21) allowing manufacture of records of musical works for retail sale.

3. Artistic works

This term includes paintings, sculptures, drawings, engravings, photographs, works of architecture and other works of artistic craftsmanship. Etchings, lithographs, woodcuts, prints, etc., count as engravings unless they are "photographs"; whilst "photograph" includes pictures produced by processes like photography. (On the other hand, part of a cinematograph film does not count as a photograph.) These details are important, because of the period of copyright: which is (subject to the proposed changes mentioned above) 50 years from publication for a photograph, 50 years from the death of the author or publication (whichever is later) for an engraving; but 50 years from the death of the author for other artistic works. (Most artistic works are never published in the copyright sense of issue of copies to the public; showing is not publication.) See below as to cinematograph films. Models of buildings, as well as buildings themselves, count as architectural works.

The acts restricted by the copyright in an artistic work are: reproduction (including reproduction of a three-dimensional work in two dimensions and—subject to the special standard mentioned previously—of a two-dimensional work in three); publication; inclusion in a television programme. There are special rules as to use of artistic works as industrial designs, discussed in this chapter and Chapter 6. There are also various exceptions, discussed in the next chapter, covering the painting, photographing, etc., of sculptures permanently situated in public, of architectural works wherever situated, or of works of artistic craftmanship which both are permanently situated in a public place and also fail to qualify as artistic works under any other head. (These exceptions also cover the publication of the paintings, photographs, etc.)

4. Cinematograph films

Films are copyright as such, not merely as a combination of a sound-track and a series of photographs—indeed, the photographs included in a film do not count as photographs for copyright purposes. The copyright belongs to whoever arranges for the making of the film: *i.e.* the producer, not the cameraman. The term "cinematograph film" is broadly defined so that (for instance) a television programme recorded on tape counts as a "film." The period of copyright is 50 years (from registration, in the case of a British film covered by the registration provisions of the Cinematograph Films Act 1938; from publication otherwise— "publication," as usual, meaning releasing copies of it, not just showing it on T.V. for instance). It has, however, been proposed that the law should be changed so that the period of 50 years runs from the time when the film is made available to the public with the consent of the copyright owner or, failing such an event within 50 years of the making of the film, from the making of the film. When the 50 years comes to an end, not only does the film lose copyright but it ceases to be an infringement of the copyright in any music included in the film, or any book or play on which the film was based, to show the film in public.

Copyright

The acts restricted by the copyright in a film are making copies of it (or, of course, of substantial parts of it); showing it in public and broadcasting it. If it is broadcast, by the B.B.C. or I.T.A., the copyright in the film is not infringed by operating a receiver in public, unless the broadcast itself was an infringement; and even then, the copyright owner must sue the broadcasting authority and not people with receivers. It is not infringement to show a newsreel more than 50 years after the time when it was taken, even though the copyright may still subsist. It is infringement to make records from the sound-track of the film (and to copy or sell the records) even though the pictures are not taken, and infringement to copy a substantial part of the picture matter even without the sound-track.

5. Sound recordings

The copyright in a sound recording belongs to the owner of the original tape on which it is made, but subject to an exception (discussed in Chap. 18) for commissioned recordings. It lasts for 50 years from publication (in the sense of issue to the public of records). Similar proposals have been made regarding the alteration of the term of protection of sound recordings as have been made in relation to cinematograph films. The acts restricted by the copyright are making records embodying the recording (and of course selling or importing them, etc.), playing it in public or broadcasting it. As with cinematograph films, if B.B.C. or I.T.A. do broadcast it, the copyright owner cannot sue anyone for operating a receiver in public; and there are special provisions allowing the playing of records in some clubs, hotels, holiday camps (*Phonographic Performance* v. *Pontin's* (1968)), etc., without special licence (this is only the copyright in the records —a licence will still be needed from the Performing Right Society to play the music on the record, if the occasion counts as " public " apart from these special provisions). The copyright is lost, if the copyright owner allows records to be sold which do not bear the date of first publication. (In the case of recordings made before June 1957, this does not apply, but copyright only lasts for 50 years from the making of the recording.)

6. Typography of published books and music

There is a separate copyright in the typography of published editions of literary, dramatic and musical works, distinct from the copyright in the works themselves. (Editions which merely reproduce the typographical arrangement of a previous edition do not count.) The copyright belongs to the publisher, and lasts for 25 years from publication. The act restricted by this copyright is reproducing the typographical arrangement of the published edition by a " photographic or similar process." The primary function of this copyright is to protect publishers of new editions of works which are no longer copyright from pirates using up-to-date copying methods.

7. Broadcasts

The B.B.C. and the I.T.A. have a special copyright in their own broadcasts, lasting for 50 years from first broadcast; this copyright restricts both re-broadcasting of the broadcast or making films and recordings of it (otherwise than for private purposes), and allowing a paying audience to see or hear it (either live or recorded). The definition of a paying audience is rather complicated.

20

WHAT IS NOT INFRINGEMENT

The Owner of the Copyright Cannot Control Legitimate Copies

Comparison of the rights of a copyright owner, discussed in the last chapter, with those of (for instance) a patentee will show that copyright is really rather limited in scope. A patentee can, by limited licensing, continue to control patented articles even after they leave his hands. The copyright owner, although given large powers of control over infringing copies and over movement of copies from one country to another, has no control within a single country over legitimate copies once they have left his hands. All he can do is to ensure that such copies are not used for the purpose of other sorts of infringement. Provided he does nothing further to the work, the owner of an authorised copy can deal with it as he pleases. An instance was pointed out in Chapter 16. An ordinary business letter being copyright, the competitor who gets hold of an indiscreet letter and distributes copies of it will infringe that copyright. But provided he got hold of the letter lawfully and properly, there is nothing to stop him circulating the original amongst his customers: a more troublesome proceeding perhaps but probably just as effective. So also, the purchaser of a painting will probably not own the copyright in it, but that only matters if he wants to copy it: he can sell or exhibit the original without troubling about copyright. It is only infringing copies of works that are dangerous in normal handling, and even then there is nothing wrong in owning such copies—provided they are treated as borrowed from and belonging to the owner of the copyright.

A good example of the inability of a copyright owner to control authorised copies is found in the campaign of paperback publishers against libraries which rebind the paperbacks instead of buying the hard-cover editions. If patents were involved a notice of limited licence would be effective to prevent this. (We ought to point out that publishers of books are able to enforce retail price maintenance on books, but this is not done by virtue of copyright law but by virtue of the restrictive trade practices law.)

No formalities are needed for " consent " to the making

What is Not Infringement

of copies or of the performing of a work. The consent must be obtained before the acts to which it applies are done: in particular, a copy made without consent is an infringing copy, and a subsequent agreement with the owner of the copyright will not alter the fact. Further, unless the consent takes the form of a proper licence (such as is considered in Chap. 21), it can be withdrawn at any time. But if, at the time when a copy was made, the making had consent, then that copy is an authorised copy and the copyright owner has no more control over it.

Specific Exceptions to the Rules for Infringement

The Copyright Act lays down a number of specific exceptions to the rules for infringement. It will be observed that several of them apply only to particular categories of " works." This limitation to particular categories is important, for a court will pay strict attention to it. Some are too special to call for discussion here; they are mentioned in the Note to the preceding chapter. Some, however, are general in application.

Fair dealing

First, copyright will not be infringed by any fair treatment of any literary, dramatic, musical or artistic work for purposes of research or private study. " Fair " here means little more than that the treatment must be genuine and reasonable for the purpose. For instance, an examination paper will be copyright; it will be an infringement for anyone to publish or copy and distribute the paper either before or after the examination concerned; but for a student to make a copy for his own purposes will not be an infringement. He will clearly be acting for the purpose of private study, and to take a single copy of such a work is probably " fair " in the sense of the Copyright Act. This in fact is a type of activity that the copyright law is not well adapted to prevent. On the other hand, to copy a large part of the work for private study, when the work is on sale and a copy could have been bought, probably would not be " fair " and so would be infringement. (There is a special provision, allowing works to be reproduced in the questions and answers of the actual examination.)

Similarly, fair dealing with such a work for purposes of criticism or review does not infringe. Here again it is the dealing with the work that has to be fair—not, for instance, the criticism of it. Any extract may be published, if its publication is genuinely intended to enable the reviewer to make his comments, and not to enable the reader of the review to enjoy the work concerned without buying it. Whether the whole of the work can properly be published in a review or criticism will depend upon circumstances: a whole short story could not be, but a critic of a "Penny Pool Table" was held entitled to set out the whole table in order effectively to comment upon it. But the review must contain an acknowledgment of the title and author of the work.

Again, there is no infringement in fair dealing with literary, musical or dramatic works for the purpose of reporting current events, either in a newspaper or magazine or in a news-reel film or broadcast (a newspaper or magazine must state the title and author of the work). What is "fair" for this purpose is less clear; in the case cited in the last chapter, about the march "Colonel Bogey," it was decided (before fair dealing was extended to news-reel films) that what was done there would not have been fair in a newspaper—that is, it would have been an infringement for a newspaper to have said: "For the benefit of those who were unable to be present yesterday, we publish the principal air of the 'Colonel Bogey' march," and then to have printed the music.

The proposals for the reform of copyright law would create a general exception in favour of "fair dealing" which does not conflict with normal exploitation of the work and does not unreasonably prejudice the legitimate interests of the copyright owner. The proposed exception would cover all classes of copyright works, and would obviate the need for separate exceptions in respect of "fair dealing" for research or private study, criticism or review, or reporting current events.

An artist re-using sketches, etc.

It is not an infringement, for the author of an artistic work who has parted with the copyright in it to make use again of preliminary sketches, models, etc., so long as he does not imitate the main design of the first work. That is to say, he may use details again, provided he does not actually copy them off the work whose copyright he has sold, but only separate details. It is of course never easy to show that an artist has infringed his own copyright, for if his style is at all

What is Not Infringement

individual, one picture of his is likely to be much like any other of a similar subject.

Photographs of works in public places

To paint, draw or photograph a building, or a piece of sculpture or suchlike work that is permanently displayed in public, is not infringement; nor is the publication of the picture. Nor is it infringement to include such a work in a film or television broadcast. There are of course restrictions on photography in many public places, but they are not copyright restrictions. The pictures themselves are of course copyright, and their reproduction would need the consent of the owner of that copyright.

Other cases

There are various provisions permitting reproduction and performance of works in the course of school lessons, and a rather limited provision permitting the publication of anthologies for school use. There are also special provisions allowing the supply by libraries of copied extracts from books and periodicals, and a provision allowing general copying, from archives, of unpublished works whose authors have been dead for more than 50 years. There are curiously limited provisions allowing works to be reproduced for the purpose of legal proceedings or of law reports. They only apply to literary, musical, dramatic and artistic works; and only permit reproduction, not performance. Thus strictly, a judge who cannot read music and accordingly must hear it played, or who wishes to listen to a gramophone record or tape recording, must close his court to the public. Probably, if he wants to be supplied with substantial extracts from a book, they must be typed out (since a photostat would reproduce and so infringe copyright in the " typographical arrangement " of the book), unless photographic copies can be obtained from an approved library. It is however proposed that the exception in favour of reproduction for the purposes of judicial proceedings, etc., should be extended to cover all classes of copyright work.

The Right to Reproduce, Subject to Royalties

In certain cases, works may be reproduced without consent provided royalties are paid to the owner of the copyright; but this is a topic belonging to Chapter 21.

21

DEALINGS IN COPYRIGHT

INTRODUCTION

THE right given by the Copyright Act to an author, of preventing other people from reproducing his works, is of very little value in itself: for his main problem in almost every case is to get himself into a position where anyone wants to reproduce his works at all. That problem is outside the scope of this book. Once it has been solved however a whole group of legal questions arise: not only formal problems of transfer of copyright, but various other questions, as to the terms on which reproduction shall take place, whether the money is to be paid to the author or the Inland Revenue, and so on. It is with questions of this type that the present chapter is concerned.

FORMAL PROBLEMS

On transfers of copyright

Copyright can be freely transferred, either as a whole or for a particular field: thus the film rights in a novel, for instance, or the performing rights in a play, can be transferred separately from the right of printing and publishing. The copyright in any country outside the United Kingdom can—so far as English law is concerned—be dealt with separately from the United Kingdom rights. But the transfer must be in writing; and a transfer is not the same as an agreement to transfer. Consider for instance the common case of a book or article commissioned by a publisher for a lump sum, on the terms that the publisher is to get the copyright. Perhaps there is a written agreement to that effect. Even so, however, the agreement will not then and there transfer the copyright: for it will be entered into before the work is created, and so there will be no copyright then in existence for it to transfer. If the agreement purports to assign the copyright, and there is nothing else wrong, and the agreement is signed on behalf of the prospective owner of the copyright, the effect will be that the copyright belongs to the publisher when it comes into existence. If not, the position will be that the author owns the copyright, but he has agreed that the publisher shall have it. Some publishers do, some do not, demand an actual assignment in such cases, though all could do so if they wished. For most purposes, the position is of course the same as if the copyright had been transferred; but if any sort of dispute arises the difference will become important. If the copyright is infringed, for instance, and the publisher wishes to sue the infringer, the action will have to be brought in the author's name, though the publisher must pay for it and will be entitled to any damages that may be recovered. Or again, suppose there is a dispute as to who is going to have the copyright, and the author (thinking himself entitled to do so, or even acting dishonestly) sells it to a second publisher who knows nothing of the agreement with the first, the second sale will be effective: the author as actual owner of the copyright could validly sell it, and the only remedy of the first publisher is to sue him for breaking his contract. (If the second publisher knew of the agreement, or even if circumstances were such that he ought to have found out about it, then he will be bound by it.)

This distinction between selling and agreeing to sell runs right through our English law of property; confusing as it is, there are many problems that cannot be understood unless it is borne in mind. In connection with the sale of a house, or something like that, few people forget that until the house has been formally conveyed to its new owner it is not his; but with intangible property like copyright this is not so easy to remember. There is a reported case for instance of the reconstruction of a company, where the old company's assets included a copyright of great value that was never actually transferred to the new company; the omission being discovered only after the old company had been dissolved. The difficulty could be, and was, overcome with the aid of the High Court; but that sort of thing costs time and money. Few companies would wind themselves up without handing over for instance the land on which their factory was built.

Foreign formalities

Where foreign copyrights are concerned, any transfer must conform to the legal requirements of the country concerned; some countries demand more and some less in the way of ceremony when property is transferred, and although an assignment valid by English law will usually suffice if it is made in England, it is seldom wise to rely on this. In America and in most Dominions, copyrights may be registered, and failure to register may involve inconvenience.

Copyright

In countries like America, which hold to rather archaic legal forms (as well as having copyright laws differing from ours) it is always unwise to try to do without native legal advice; and even in Canada, for instance (where by and large legal documents in English form would be effective) it will be found that an assignment is not fully effective until after registration. Of course, those who are much involved in copyright matters (cinematograph companies and music publishers, for instance) have rule-of-thumb methods for handling foreign copyright problems which seem usually to work well enough.

On licensing

An owner of copyright who does not want to transfer it outright may license it: that is to say, may grant to someone else the right to do acts that would normally infringe that copyright. Again, the licence must be in writing; and here also there is a distinction that must be watched—that between a licence and a mere consent to the doing of certain acts. There is never any infringement involved in reproducing a copyright work, if the owner of the copyright consents; but a true licence carries with it a right of property in a way that a mere consent does not. Thus a true licence can give rights enforceable against the owner himself (in case he should change his mind) or against anyone to whom he sells the copyright, whilst an exclusive licensee can sue infringers. A mere consent on the other hand can be withdrawn by the copyright owner, or overridden by a sale of the copyright, leaving the other party with nothing except (possibly) a right to sue for breach of contract. Licences require no special formalities in English law; like transfers of copyright, so long as they are in writing and it is clear what they mean, no special words or forms are needed. (The document must, however, be properly stamped.)

On sound recordings of musical works

The Copyright Act contains a rather unusual provision about sound recordings of musical works. If the owner of the copyright in a musical work once allows records of it to be manufactured here (or to be imported into this country), any United Kingdom record manufacturer who likes can record it again on payment of a royalty fixed by the Department of Trade. The provision only applies to records for retail sale, does not authorise the recording of adaptations of a work (unless the copyright owner has previously authorised recording of a similar adaptation) and authorises only recordings made in this country—it does not authorise the importation either of records or of tapes from which records are nowadays made. Where words go with the music, the right to record covers them too; but spoken records as such are outside the scope of the provision. Few composers object to recording of their works, and the main importance of this provision is that it sets a standard royalty rate that the owners of musical copyrights cannot force the gramophone companies to exceed, except where the records (or the " tapes " they are made from) are imported from abroad.

Contracts Relating to Copyrights

Apart from the points already mentioned in this chapter, dealings in copyright are entirely a matter for contract—that is to say, those concerned may make what rules they please. What has happened in relation to any particular copyright must consequently be deduced from such agreements, formal or informal, as the parties have made; this may be a matter of very great difficulty. It should in particular be assumed that any agreement drawn up by business men will prove difficult for lawyers (including judges) to sort out; for lawyers and business men have quite different ideas both as to the way they use language and as to the sort of things that agreements ought to provide for. It is however possible to lay down a few general rules as to what the position is likely to be if the parties have said nothing definite to the contrary.

Implied terms

In all cases it has to be remembered that the law is very chary of reading into agreements terms that the parties have not actually stated. The rule is: Such terms will only be implied if the agreement cannot be effective without them, so that there can be no doubt that if when the contract was made the parties had been asked whether this was what they wanted, they would both have said " Yes, of course." For example, if there is a sale of a copyright work of art, such as a picture, the copyright will not be transferred with the work unless the parties agree that it shall. This is obvious in the case of a work with many copies, like a coloured print; it is not so obvious in the case of something like a painting of which only the original exists. But if the parties are silent as to the copyright, the law will not assume that they meant

Copyright

to transfer it unless it is clear that this must have been so. In the case, say, of a sale of a painting to a maker of Christmas cards, if both parties knew that he meant to make a Christmas card of it, it will be clear that they must have meant that he should have some right to reproduce the painting; but even then, it does not necessarily follow that he must have the ownership of the copyright rather than a licence to reproduce. In any event, unless there is something in writing he will get merely a contractual right to have the copyright assigned to him or a licence granted to him, as the case may be.

Where works are made to order

It was pointed out in Chapter 18 that special rules cover works created by employees, and also portraits, photographs, engravings and sound recordings made to order: that is, the employer or the person giving the order (as the case may be) gets the copyright from the beginning. Where works of other sorts are produced to order, although the author gets the copyright in the first instance, it will often be clear (if not expressly stated) that the parties meant the copyright to be transferred to the person giving the order; a term in their agreement to that effect will then be implied. For instance, where a publisher commissions a book for a lump sum payment, even if nothing is said about copyright it will normally be assumed that the publisher is meant to have it. The author is not an employee, so as to make the publisher the first owner of the copyright: this is shown by the fact that the publisher cannot tell him how to write his book but must take it as the author thinks it should be written. Nevertheless, for a lump sum payment the publisher presumably expected to get the whole thing, copyright and all. (But remember that there will only be an agreement to transfer the copyright to the publisher, not an actual transfer, unless a signed agreement says it is a transfer.) On the other hand if payment is to be by royalty there will be no reason to suppose that the publisher is necessarily to have more than a licence to publish; and in the case of an architectural work for instance, even if specially commissioned, the only term as to copyright which will be implied into the contract is a licence to the architect's client to erect the buildings contracted for in accordance with the drawings. The architect will therefore keep his copyright. A clear case the other way was of a man who was commissioned to do the choreography for a ballet:

Dealings in Copyright

clearly the copyright must have been intended to be transferred to the man who commissioned the work, for without that copyright he would not have a complete ballet.

Bequests of copyright works

In one case the Copyright Act itself creates a presumption that copyright goes with the property in the actual work: where an artistic work, or the manuscript of a literary, musical or dramatic work, is bequeathed by a will which does not mention the copyright. (Of course, this only applies so far as the testator owned the copyright when he died.)

Where a publisher agrees to publish an author's work

There are cases however where it is clear that the parties must have intended to provide for quite a number of matters they have said nothing about. For instance, an author may send the manuscript of a book to a publisher and the publisher agree to publish it, and nothing else be said at all. In that case the law will imply, grudgingly, the bare minimum of terms to complete the contract. The publisher has a licence to publish an edition of the book, but that is all: the author of course keeps the ownership of the copyright. The publisher must pay the author a reasonable royalty: not necessarily the royalty he usually pays, rather the sort of royalty an ordinary publisher would normally pay for that sort of book. The publisher must publish an edition of the book, of reasonable size having regard to all the circumstances, within a reasonable time. A reasonable time for publishing a book in these days will be many months, and there would certainly be no obligation upon the publisher to hurry unduly; but he must not deliberately delay. He must not for instance, as a publisher once did, deliberately delay publication so as to enable a rival to scoop the Christmas market with a book on the same subject—in return of course for a share of the profits on his rival's book. Finally he is not entitled to publish the book under someone else's name as author: the position would however be different if he had bought the copyright outright, then he could probably deal with the work as he pleased.

In the same way, if a manuscript is sent to the editor of a periodical the editor may publish it, and must pay at reasonable rates. His usual rates will usually do, and will certainly do if the author has taken them before: but a periodical which usually pays unusually low rates should tell new authors about them before publication, or it may

Copyright

find that the court considers them unreasonable. The editor of a periodical is not entitled to publish in book form manuscripts sent to him for periodical publication, without the author's consent.

Sales of part of a copyright

The same sort of considerations arise when a copyright is partially sold; but here the position tends to be clearer, for the parties must have said something about what they intend shall happen, and all the lawyers have to decide is what the parties' words mean. (The answer may surprise the parties, but that often happens to those who are insufficiently explicit in the first place.) Thus the sale of the performing rights in a play or a song will not pass the right to make films or gramophone records of the work, unless there is some special reason why the parties must have meant this to be so; but it will pass the right to prevent any film or record of the book being shown or played in public. This will be vital in the case of a play to be made into a film, which is almost certainly intended for public exhibition (unless perhaps it is meant solely for export to a country where either there is no copyright or the performing right has not been sold); but it will be less important to the maker of a gramophone record. Gramophone records as normally sold are in fact not licensed for public performance, and every English record at least bears a notice to that effect.

Performing right societies

What actually happens with musical copyrights is that the performing rights in published music are all handed over to the Performing Right Society, and the performing rights in records to a similar society set up by the record companies. In the case of films including previously published music, the film company buys a licence to include the music in the film (there are standard arrangements for this), but does not have authority to license public performance of it. The cinema theatre has a standard Performing Right Society licence which covers that.

The film distributor, in effect, warrants that an exhibitor will have no copyright trouble, provided his cinemas have Performing Right Society licences (that is to say, the film company is expected to look after performing rights in any book or play the film is made from, but not performing rights in music except music specially written for the film). The actual agreements used in the film industry tend to be rather incomprehensible, but custom has established what they are supposed to mean.

People wanting to use gramophone records for public performance go to the two societies and obtain standard licences: one covering the copyright in music, one covering that in the recording. There is a Performing Right Tribunal with power to see that the standard licences are not unreasonable.

Where the ownership of the manuscript and copyright is in different hands

A case similar to overlapping copyrights arises where the owner of an unpublished manuscript does not own the copyright in it. He cannot publish it without the copyright owner's consent, but then the copyright owner cannot get at the manuscript without his consent: so that again an intending publisher must come to terms with both.

Publishing agreements

Two odd points relating to publishing agreements deserve notice. Such agreements often contain a clause requiring the author to offer his next book (or next so many books) to the same publisher. This is a perfectly legitimate clause for a contract to contain, and can be enforced: a court will grant an injunction not only to prevent the author disposing of those books elsewhere, but also to prevent another publisher, who took those books although he knew about the agreement, from publishing them. On the other hand, an agreement to write a number of further books would not be enforceable by injunction: injunctions are not given to compel the performance of personal services.

The second point is more difficult. Suppose the author, not being under any obligation to offer his next book to the same publisher, writes another on the same subject and offers it to a second publisher, who publishes it and so spoils the market for the first: has the first publisher any remedy? Or suppose the publisher puts out a second book on the same subject at the same time, and so spoils the first author's sales: has the author any remedy? The answer will of course depend on what the publishing agreement says, and since the publisher will very likely have drawn it up it will probably protect him against the author but not the author against him. If the agreement is altogether silent on the subject, it seems fairly clear that in an ordinary case the

Copyright

author would have no remedy; probably the publisher would have none either, but this is not quite so clear.

Literary agents

It is usual for established authors at least to employ literary agents to place their books and deal with the various forms of copyright arising from them. Here again, the rights of the author and his agent as against each other are what they have agreed them to be when the agent took the job. It should be remembered however that as against the outside world, the agent's powers to deal on behalf of his principal will in effect be those that such agents usually have. The author can, if he likes and the agent is willing, make special terms and place special restrictions on the agent's authority; but the special terms and restrictions will have no effect against third parties who do not know of them.

Manuscripts sent for advice

It is not unusual for authors who are not established to send their works to their more successful brethren for comment, advice, and assistance in placing with publishers or producers. The rights of the author in such a case are clear. The man he sends his manuscript to must not of course publish it (though he may be expected to show it to one or two colleagues), nor may he copy from it: but he is under no obligation to take any particular care of it, and if it gets lost or damaged the author should not complain.

TAXATION AND AUTHORS

The question of tax upon author's earnings, important as it is, can be dealt with here only very briefly. The position is broadly this. Any author who makes a business or profession of writing or composing, or anyone who makes a business of dealing in copyrights, must pay income tax on the whole profits of that business, whether they are received in the form of royalties or of lump-sum payments. Those who do not make a business of it, like casual authors or people who happen to have come into possession of an odd copyright, must pay income tax on receipts if they are income but not if they are capital. It does not necessarily follow that royalties are income, though they usually are; still less does it follow that lump-sum payments are capital. The test is more or less this: was there a valuable asset, and has it been converted into money (in which case the proceeds of conversion will

Dealings in Copyright

be capital) or has it been used as a source of profit—as an income-bearing investment, so to speak? If it has, that profit will be income. A sale of an existing copyright, by someone who has never written a book before, whether for a single payment or annual payments, may be capital, and not taxable unless it is the profit of a business; on the other hand a royalty of so much a copy on the sales of a book is almost certainly income, even if it is paid as a lump sum when the agreement is made. If a work is commissioned, the payment is almost certain to be received as income whatever form it takes: for essentially it is payment for services, not the sale of any asset. It will be seen that the author of a really successful work will find some difficulty in arranging his affairs so as to avoid paying out in one or two years of extremely high income, almost the whole of what he gets for it. However, such an author can, to a reasonable extent, " spread " out (for tax purposes) payments he receives, over a longer period, provided he spent over a year in writing the work.

22
CONFIDENCE AND COPYRIGHT

INTRODUCTION

THE present chapter deals with a matter in some way akin to copyright disputes (though it does not depend on Acts of Parliament): the right not to stop others from reproducing a work, but to stop them making use of the information contained in it. This is a job which the ownership of copyright will seldom do. Thus it will be recalled that a purchaser of a book is entitled to read it and let anyone else read it, and even to recite bits of it in public to anyone who will listen. No limitation by way of limited licence can be imposed by the owner of the copyright if the copy is an authorised copy; even if the copy is not authorised all the copyright owner can do is to insist upon the handing over of the book to him—what he cannot do by virtue of his ownership of the copyright is to prevent readers of the book making use of what they learnt by reading it.

The sort of problems dealt with in this chapter generally, although not always, arise in commercial matters: with the inventor who shows his invention to others before his patents have been granted or even (inventors are not always cautious people) before he has applied for patents at all; the manufacturer who supplies manufacturing drawings and specifications to a sub-contractor; the merchant who gives the names and addresses of customers to the manufacturer so that they can be supplied direct. In all cases of this sort, what the man who supplied the information really wants is to stop the recipient of the information from using it except for the purpose for which it was given. A mere right to stop the recipient from making copies, which is given by copyright, is useful but is not enough.

THE ACTION FOR BREACH OF CONFIDENCE

The general rule

The right needed by a supplier of confidential information is given by the law, but only in certain circumstances and subject to certain exceptions. The general rule has been put in the following way, namely, that a recipient of confidential information may not use that information

Confidence and Copyright

without the consent of the man he got it from (*Saltman Engineering* v. *Campbell Engineering* (1948)). Another way in which the rule has been expressed is that a plaintiff who sues for breach of confidence must show three things: first, that the information has the necessary quality of confidence about it; secondly, that the information was imparted in circumstances importing an obligation of confidence; and thirdly, that there was an unauthorised use made of that information (*Coco* v. *Clark* (1969)). The judge who decided the latter case thought that it was possible that the plaintiff would also have to show that he was personally prejudiced by the unauthorised use of the information, but did not decide the point.

When is information confidential?

(*a*) *Circumstances giving rise to a relationship of confidence*

These can be shortly stated: a person can be prevented from misusing information given to him if, when he receives it, he has agreed, expressly or impliedly, to treat it as confidential. This does not mean that there has to be a formal agreement, although of course having such an agreement helps to make the position clear to everyone (which is why the cases which are fought are mostly concerned with situations where the parties did not make it clear that their relationship was confidential from the outset). What the judges do in cases where there is no express agreement is to look at all the circumstances surrounding the relationship between the parties. If it appears that the parties cannot have intended the information to be given freely, then it was given in confidence. A lot may depend upon how the judge feels about the way the defendant behaved. If information is given for a particular purpose, it is easily inferred that the parties intended the information to be used only for that purpose. A few examples will make the point clearer.

In *Seager* v. *Copydex* (1967) an inventor had discussed an invention of his with the defendant company with a view to their taking it up. In the course of the discussion he mentioned the idea behind another invention he had in mind. Although the company did not take up the first invention, they later came out with a version of the second, even using the name which the inventor had given it. The Court of Appeal thought the defendants must have taken the inventor's idea, albeit subconsciously, and that the relationship between the parties must have been confidential

Copyright

since the inventor could not be supposed to have been giving the information freely; it was given merely for the purpose of interesting the defendants in his ideas.

Again, in *Ackroyds* v. *Islington Plastics* (1962) the defendants had been under contract to manufacture plastic " swizzle sticks " (things for getting those nasty bubbles out of champagne) for the plaintiffs. The plaintiffs had supplied the defendants for this purpose with information and with a special tool. It was held that the defendants could not use either the information or the tool for the purpose of manufacturing swizzle sticks for themselves: both had been handed over only for the purpose of helping them manufacture for the plaintiffs.

One other example shows that the law of confidence, although generally finding its application in the commercial field, is perfectly general. In *Argyll* v. *Argyll* (1965) the then Duchess of Argyll sued to prevent the Duke from supplying to a Sunday newspaper (and to prevent the Sunday newspaper from publishing) what the Duke had said to her in confidence during their marriage, which had ended in divorce a little earlier. The judge said that the marriage relationship was in its nature confidential and that the obligations of confidence continued after the marriage had ended.

(b) The effect of marking things " confidential "

We have said that the test of confidentiality is the express or implied intention of the parties. It follows that marking a document " confidential " will not make it so, if the man who receives it does not know, and has no reason to expect, that it is to be confidential. If you see a book advertised for sale and send up the money and get a copy of the book back, the book is already yours before you unpack it or look at it. It may turn out to be highly confidential and labelled so, but that makes no difference: you did not agree not to disclose its contents when you offered to buy it and you need not agree now. On the other hand, if the book is stated in the advertisement to be confidential, only for your personal use, then in replying to the advertisement you agree to keep it as confidential and must keep to your contract—even if on investigation the book turns out to be something you could buy at any bookstall or—as in one decided case—an explanation of a system for betting on horse-races according to the phases of the moon.

Confidence and Copyright

(c) Confidence and contract

Where parties are in a contractual relationship they often provide for obligations of confidence in express terms. Thus normally no scientist will be employed by the research department of a company unless he agrees to keep the company information secret even after he leaves the company. But even where there is no such express obligation, the relationship between the parties may of its nature give rise to obligations of confidence: as in the "swizzlestick" case mentioned above, or in *Robb* v. *Green* (1895) where an ex-employee was restrained from using a list of his old employer's customers for his own benefit. The point is that the law of confidence exists apart from the law of contract, but when obligations of confidence exist there is usually some contractual relationship between the parties.

(d) What happens where the information becomes public knowledge

Suppose that by the time the action comes to trial the information concerned has been either wholly or partly made available to the public. What then?

At first sight it would seem absurd that a defendant should be under any restriction in using information which is public knowledge. But things are not so simple: a defendant may obtain a considerable advantage from information which, when it was supplied to him, was confidential but which has now become public knowledge—one judge expressed this sort of situation vividly by saying that such a defendant was using the information as a "springboard for activities detrimental to the plaintiff."

At present the law upon this subject is not clear. On the one hand it has been held that a man who lets all the information be disclosed by publication of his patent specification can no longer prevent ex-employees from revealing that information. On the other hand it is also clear that the courts are willing to give some relief to a plaintiff who shows that the defendant has obtained an unfair advantage by using the plaintiff's confidential information as a "springboard" even when the information has later become public. The courts say that, in such cases, although it is true that the information was available from public sources, the defendant did not get it from them, but got it from the "tainted source" of the plaintiff's confidential disclosure to him. Once a defendant is under the suspicion that he has used a "tainted source" he may find himself in difficulty.

Copyright

It may then be no use his saying "Look, I know I had dealings with the plaintiff in the past which were confidential, but I developed this machine by myself and here are my plans to prove it." The court may still feel he got the idea from the plaintiff and find a breach of confidence. *Seager* v. *Copydex* is just such a case. Another example is afforded by the manufacturer who has a list of the customers of the merchant for whom he makes goods. In the sort of field where this point is most likely to arise it may be that anyone could compile a pretty good list of customers and potential customers from trade directories and the like. Nevertheless, let such a manufacturer once show a disposition to take unfair advantage of his position and he may find himself forbidden to approach those customers at all.

The difficulties in this concept of the "springboard" case are well described in the judgment in *Coco* v. *Clark*.

Remedies

The remedies for a breach of confidence are much the same as those granted for the infringement of the other rights discussed in this book (see Chap. 1). Thus injunctions can be, and often are, awarded, together with damages or accounts of profits. In some cases the court will not award an injunction but will award damages only. This occurred in *Seager* v. *Copydex* where, since the information was, at the time of the action, publicly known and the plaintiff's information was only a part of the information being used by the defendants, an injunction was thought to be inappropriate and damages enough to compensate the plaintiff. In fact there followed a dispute as to the way in which damages should be calculated and the matter had to go to the Court of Appeal again upon this question (*Seager* v. *Copydex* (1969)). The court held that damages should be paid upon the market value of the information, which depended upon how important it was: whether, for example, it was inventive enough to support a patent, or was merely the sort of information which could have been supplied by any expert.

Interlocutory injunctions

If the plaintiff acts quickly enough he will in a suitable case be granted an interlocutory injunction: where the information concerned is not yet public, for instance, to preserve the status quo while the case is fought. But in

" springboard " cases it seems that the courts are unwilling to grant such injunctions, partly because the questions of fact as to exactly how much of the information used by the defendant was taken from the plaintiff and how much the defendants got for themselves are too difficult to resolve without hearing all the evidence, and partly because, in such cases, the plaintiff may in the end, if he wins, receive only damages. *Coco* v. *Clark* (1969) is an example of such a refusal. (But note that the judge, whilst refusing the interlocutory injunction, thought that the defendants ought, pending the trial, to pay a potential royalty into a bank account so that if the plaintiff eventually won the action, he would be safeguarded, and an undertaking to this effect was given to the court.)

Suing third parties

If the owner of the information is able to act before it has been disclosed to any third party, then an injunction preventing disclosure should be all he needs to protect it. If it has already been passed on to a third party, an injunction will not be much good unless it binds the third party too. Anyone who receives information that he knows (or ought to know) reached him through a breach of confidence has a duty not to use or disclose it, and the court will in a proper case grant an injunction to enforce that duty. Thus in the *Argyll* case mentioned above, not only the Duke was placed under an injunction but also the Sunday newspaper which was going to print the information.

The exact limits to the circumstances in which third parties can be sued are not yet fully worked out because there have not been many cases on the subject. However, the law is probably that where someone pays for the information in good faith then he cannot be stopped from using it. It would be different if he acted in bad faith (for example where a company has bought information from someone they knew to be an industrial spy or an employee of another company) and it may be different if he does not pay for it.

Problems of proof

From what has been said, it might be thought that the law gave enough protection to confidential information to make disclosure of it perfectly safe. Any such idea would be entirely wrong. As always, neither the general law nor even a carefully drawn contract is any real protection against dishonesty. The function of these things—of a

Copyright

proper contract especially—is to make it clear, amongst honest parties to a transaction, just what they may and may not do. The only remedy against rogues is to have nothing to do with them.

If a would-be plaintiff does come up against a rogue then he will find it difficult to prove his case. The burden will lie on him to show he gave the rogue confidential information in circumstances giving rise to a bond of confidence and that the rogue is using such information. In some cases the would-be plaintiff will not even know that the rogue is using the information. For example, suppose a company learns from an employee of another company that a particular line of research has been tried and found useless. This will save the first company from trying that line, but the company from whom the information was "taken" will have very little chance of proving that the other company acted in breach of confidence. When it comes to information passed on to third parties the problems of proof grow even harder.

Where the action will not lie

(*a*) " *No confidence in a guilty secret* "

Since the action for breach of confidence is founded originally upon what is fair, the courts will not grant a remedy if the information which the defendant threatens to reveal or use is something which ought not, in conscience, to be protected. Thus, for example, in *Initial Towel Services* v. *Putterill* (1967) the plaintiffs failed to obtain interlocutory injunctions against an ex-employee and a daily newspaper when the ex-employee alleged that the information he was giving to the newspaper showed that the plaintiffs had been a party to a secret arrangement to keep prices up, contrary to the Restrictive Trade Practices Act.

(*b*) *Public policy*

There are some cases where, as a matter of public policy, agreements for confidence will not be enforced. The most important of these is in relation to skilled employees who leave their firm and propose to enter employment in the same field, perhaps with a rival manufacturer. The court will enforce covenants in restraint of trade, preventing the ex-employee from working for the competitor, provided that the covenant is not too broad in terms of the geographical area to which it extends and the time for which it operates. The court goes further, and, whether or not there is a covenant in restraint of trade in his contract of employment, will prevent an employee or ex-employee from disclosing the industrial or commercial secrets of his employer. What the court will not do, however, is to prevent him from using the general skill and knowledge (as opposed to confidential information) which he has acquired by reason of his employment. Obviously the distinction between these two is a hard one to draw in some cases, but it must be drawn, for otherwise skilled employees would never be able to change their jobs. So important do the courts regard the ability of a skilled man to do his job that even an express agreement seeking to bind the employee not to use such general knowledge will be held invalid—although that does not mean that the employee will be free to disclose company secrets.

The position of directors deserves special mention: any information obtained by a director by virtue of his office is, in effect, held on trust for the company, and must only be used for the purposes of the company. Since the directors are responsible for the conduct of the business of the company, it is seldom open to them to say that they were not told and did not realise that the information acquired was confidential.

(c) The duty of confidence must be owed to the plaintiff

In *Fraser* v. *Evans* (1969) the plaintiff sought to restrain by interlocutory injunction publication in a newspaper of parts of a confidential report he had prepared for the Greek Government. It was held that although the report was confidential and although the copyright belonged to the plaintiff, he could not succeed. He failed as to infringement of copyright since it appeared very likely that, at the trial, a defence of fair dealing (see Chap. 20) would succeed; and he failed as to breach of confidence because the report belonged to the Greek Government and not to him. Only the person to whom the duty of confidence is owed can sue to enforce it.

Sales of " Know-How "

It is not uncommon, in these days, for know-how to be treated as an article of commerce—to be sold outright, like any other property, or to be handed over on terms like those of a patent licence. Even an actual patent licence may often turn out, in reality, to be largely a dealing in know-how—it is often the know-how that is worth the

Copyright

money, rather than the more-or-less dubious monopoly given by any patent. This sort of transaction presents no very great difficulty (at least, until questions of taxation arise) in the ordinary case where both parties are honest. The agreements governing such transactions deal in detail with the degree of "confidence" to be attached to the information handed over, and especially with the position after the agreement comes to an end. This sort of transaction is rather outside the scope of the present chapter, which is more concerned with cases in which there is no express agreement laying down conditions as to confidence.

THE NEED FOR AGREEMENTS

It is always better to have questions of confidence properly covered by agreement, than to leave them to implications of the general law. Consider once again the case of a manufacturer trying out an invention. Everything may go well, in which case there will be no difficulty. But suppose the inventor's ideas turn out in the end to be more-or-less unworkable. The manufacturer may then drop the whole scheme; but suppose that in the course of finding out that the invention will not work he finds out what is wrong, and so becomes able to make something that will work. What is to be the position then? The manufacturer, especially if he has paid for the right to have first go at the invention, will feel that he has taken from the inventor nothing he has not paid for, that the new ideas are his own and that he owes the inventor nothing. The inventor will probably feel that the manufacturer is either merely being difficult, or merely making undesirable alterations in the original scheme so as to get out of paying a proper royalty. If a fight is to be avoided, there ought to be an agreement which will make it clear exactly what the manufacturer is entitled to keep if he rejects the original invention, and just exactly when a royalty or purchase price is in the end to be payable.

DIFFICULT CASES

Of course, there are difficulties no agreement can provide against; especially as neither inventors nor manufacturers are always as sensible and co-operative as they might be. For instance, if a manufacturer can be interested at all in an invention put up to him, the reason is likely to be that the problem it sets out to solve is one he knew of and had even been dabbling at himself. His reaction to seeing an outsider's proposal is likely to be that he rejects it but is encouraged to go back to his own ideas and make them work—perhaps with a bit of help from the alternative proposals that the outside inventor has put to him. Inevitably, in most such cases, the inventor will be convinced that the manufacturer has "really" stolen his invention, and the manufacturer will be convinced that he has merely pursued (as he "really" always meant to) his own previous line of development. They will never agree on the facts, and may have to ask a court to decide between them. If a proper agreement is made between them, before the invention is disclosed, this should serve to limit the range of the dispute, and so will save time, costs and some bitterness, if nothing else; but even so a dispute may be inevitable. It is worth examining in some detail the factors that make disputes so difficult to avoid in many matters of confidence.

The instance just given suggests one factor: that much information seems very much more valuable to the man giving it than to the man listening. Only too often, the man imparting industrial know-how is a crashing bore. Another factor is well illustrated by the case suggested earlier, of a merchant who lets his suppliers know the names of his customers. The real trouble here is, that the merchant's position is inherently a risky one; sooner or later, it will pay his suppliers or his customers to cut him out, and what seems to them an ordinary change in business procedure will look to him like dirty work. He will look on a list of customers or suppliers as something of great value, since to him it is; but to others, such a list is worth precisely what it would cost to pay a girl to compile it from business directories. So often what really matters is not some trade secret but just trade habits that nobody bothers to alter. The same thing can happen with industrial know-how: the difference between making something well and making it badly can be a matter of secret knowledge, but is more often a matter of skilled management and skilled labour. If a good man gets a job somewhere else at higher pay, and his new employer's products jump ahead in quality, it is easy to assume that some secret has gone with him; but the odds are that secrets played very little part in the matter. So one gets a sort of typical case, where the defendant has been rather careless over the plaintiff's confidence, not thinking it mattered much;

Copyright

and the plaintiff is over-suspicious, not realising that any competent man in the defendant's position could do the job without anybody's secrets. Both parties are sure they are 90 per cent. in the right: and the result can easily be litigation, whose outcome will be anyone's guess. There is industrial espionage, even in this country; and there are people who deliberately set out to steal their employer's secrets; but most litigation, in this field as in any other, is between people who just did not think enough.

INDEX

"A" REGISTRATION OF TRADE MARK, 57, 68, 95
ACCEPTANCE OF PATENT SPECIFICATION, 27
ACCESSORIES,
 use of trade mark for, 64
ACCOUNT OF PROFITS, 9, 166
ACTION FOR CONVERSION. *See* CONVERSION.
ACTION FOR INFRINGEMENT, 4, 30, 41, 42, 47, 51, 58, 61
 costs, 4, 5, 41
 damages, 8
 prosecution, compared with, 59, 109, 110
 remedies generally, 3
 timing, 4
ADAPTATION, 139
 musical works, 139, 144, 146
 reproduction of works, 138
ADDITION, PATENT OF, 42
ADVERTISEMENT OF TRADE MARK APPLICATION, 74
AGENTS,
 literary, 160
 patent and trade mark, 25, 31, 71
AMBIGUITY OF PATENT SPECIFICATION, 27
AMENDMENT OF PATENT SPECIFICATION, 39
ANONYMOUS WORKS, 125, 131
APPEALS FROM PATENT OFFICE,
 patent cases, 23
 trade mark cases, 74, 75
APPLICATION,
 patent, 18, 35
  See also PATENT APPLICATION.
 trade mark, 71 *et seq.*
  See also TRADE MARK APPLICATION.
ARCHITECTURAL WORKS, 117, 128, 151
 remedies for infringement, 143
ARTISTIC WORK, 49, 50, 112, 113, 125, 141, 144
 craftsmanship, 50, 118
 publication of, 145
 sketches for, 150

ASSIGNMENT,
 copyright, 152–154
 future copyright, 152
 patent, 25
 trade mark, 84
ASSOCIATED TRADE MARKS, 76, 90
AUTHOR, 137
 employee, 129
 liability for infringement, 142
 owner of copyright; when not, 126 *et seq.*
 photograph, of, 127
 recording, of, 127
 reproduction of work by, 128, 150
 taxation, 160

"B" REGISTRATION OF TRADE MARK, 57 *et seq.*, 67, 74, 81, 82
BEST METHOD OF WORKING INVENTION, 27
BROADCAST,
 copyright in, 141, 147
 infringement by 141, 147
 public performance, and, 141
 recordings, from, 147

CERTIFICATE OF CONTESTED VALIDITY,
 patent, 41
 trade mark, 66
CERTIFICATION TRADE MARK, 94 *et seq.*, 111
CHEMICAL COMPOUNDS,
 patents for, 21, 45
 trade marks for, 89
CLAIMS OF PATENT SPECIFICATION, 18 *et seq.*, 27, 35, 40
CLASSIFICATION,
 goods, 71
 works, 118, 144–147
"COLONEL BOGEY," 135, 150
COLOURS, TRADE MARK, 62
COMPANY NAME,
 passing off by, 57, 99, 103
 trade mark registration, 70
COMPILATIONS, COPYRIGHT IN, 123, 135
COMPLETE PATENT SPECIFICATION, 18, 27, 35 *et seq.*

173

Index

COMPUTER PROGRAMMES, 18
CONFIDENTIAL INFORMATION, 114, 162 et seq.
    contract and, 164
    guilty secret, 168
    public knowledge, 165
    third parties, 167
" CONNECTION IN THE COURSE OF TRADE," 68, 84
CONVENTION, EUROPEAN, 29
CONVERSION IN COPYRIGHT CASES, 8, 143
COPYRIGHT, 2, 12, 13, 48–52, 112 et seq.
    assignment, 152–154
    broadcast, in, 141, 147
    compilations, in, 123, 135
    design, in, 2, 12, 48–52
    duration, 13, 115, 144 et seq.
    film, 139
    foreign law, 117, 153
    industrial monopolies, relation to, 2, 12, 48–52
    infringement of. See INFRINGEMENT OF COPYRIGHT.
    International Convention, 117
    licence, 149, 154
    ownership. See OWNER OF COPYRIGHT.
    reforms, proposed, 130, 150
    title, in, 126 et seq.
    typographical, 146
CRIMINAL PROVISIONS, 108 et seq.
CROWN COPYRIGHT, 125, 130
CROWN USE OF INVENTIONS, 53 et seq.

DAMAGES, 8
    conversion in copyright cases, 8, 143
    innocent infringer, 9
DECLARATION AS TO NON-INFRINGEMENT OF PATENT, 42, 47
DEFENSIVE TRADE MARK REGISTRATION, 80, 98
DESCRIPTION,
    false, 108 et seq.
    trade mark infringement and, 65
DESCRIPTIVE TRADE MARKS, 69, 70, 79, 88
DESIGN,
    copyright in, 2, 12, 48–52
    registration, 2, 12, 14, 52
    trade mark, as, 70

" DESIGNING ROUND " PATENT, 11, 30, 43, 44
DISTINCTIVENESS OF TRADE MARK, 69 et seq., 88
DRAMATIC WORKS, 117, 122, 139, 140, 144
DRUGS. See CHEMICAL COMPOUNDS.
DURATION OF RIGHTS,
    copyright, 13, 115, 144 et seq.
    design registration, 14
    patent, 13, 24

EMPLOYEE,
    author, 129
    award for, 28
    inventor, 18, 27
EUROPEAN ECONOMIC COMMUNITY,
    competition policy, 86
EUROPEAN LAW, 7, 86
EUROPEAN PATENT OFFICE, 37
EXAMINATION OF PATENT APPLICATION, 23, 31, 37, 38
" EXCLUSIVE RIGHT," 3, 4, 60
EXHAUSTION OF RIGHTS, 33
EXTENSION OF TERM OF PATENT, 4–7

FALSE TRADE DESCRIPTION AND MARKS, 108 et seq.
FEES,
    patent, 24
    trade mark registration, 71
FILM COPYRIGHT, 139, 145
FILM MUSIC, 135, 158
FOOD, PATENT FOR, 21
FOREIGN LAW, 7
    copyright, 117, 153
    patent, 16 et seq., 28
    trade mark, 83, 86
FOREIGN PATENTING, 17, 36
FOREIGN TRADE MARKS, 91

GET-UP, 57, 98
" GOODS OF THE SAME DESCRIPTION," 60, 88
GOODWILL, 54, 84
GOVERNMENT PUBLICATIONS, 125, 130
GOVERNMENT USE OF INVENTIONS, ETC., 53 et seq.
GUILTY SECRET, 168

" HEARING " AT PATENT OFFICE, 23, 74

Index

ILLEGAL AND IMMORAL INVENTIONS, 27
IMPORTATION,
 infringing works, of, 86, 143
IMPROVEMENTS, PATENTING OF, 43, 44
INCOME TAX,
 author, 161
 foreign patentee, 44
 inventor, 44
 royalties, 44
INDECENT WORKS, 123
INDUSTRIAL DESIGN. *See* DESIGN *and* REGISTERED DESIGNS.
INFRINGEMENT. *See* ACTION FOR INFRINGEMENT. *And see below.*
INFRINGEMENT OF COPYRIGHT, 49, 112, 132 *et seq.*
 authorising, 142, 144
 broadcast, by, 141, 147
 copying and, 14, 112, 115, 132
 drawings, by copying from, 51, 138
 exceptions, 149 *et seq.*
 innocent, 8
 performance, by, 140, 144
 permitting, 142, 144
 proving, 50, 133
 publication of work, by, 140, 144 *et seq.*
 remedies, 4–6, 8–10
INFRINGEMENT OF PATENT, 14, 17, 30, 46, 47
 declaration as to non-, 42
 innocent, 8
 remedies, 3 *et seq.*
INFRINGEMENT OF TRADE MARK, 58, 61 *et seq.*
 passing off and, 57
 remedies, 3 *et seq.*
 test for, 67
INFRINGING WORKS,
 dealings with, 143, 144
 importation of, 143
 liability of author, 142
INITIALS AS TRADE MARKS, 70, 81
INJUNCTION, 4, 55, 166
 damages in lieu of, 167
 interlocutory, 6–7, 55, 167
INSTRUCTIONS, 19
INTERNATIONAL CONVENTIONS,
 Copyright, 117
 Industrial Property, 18
INVENTED WORD AS TRADE MARK, 69, 81, 90, 110

INVENTION,
 best definition of working, 27
 Crown use of, 53 *et seq.*
 employees', 27
 government use of, 53 *et seq.*
 illegal and immoral, 27
 novelty, of, 11, 22, 26
 obtaining of, 26
 obviousness of, 22, 26
 patentability of, 21
 prior publication of, 23, 27
 utility of, 27
INVENTOR,
 definition, 18
 employee, 18, 27
 taxation, 44

JOINT OWNERSHIP,
 patent, 32
 trade mark, 73

"KNOW-HOW," 36, 169
KOJAK, 102

LIBEL,
 trade, 105 *et seq.*
LICENCE,
 compulsory, 43, 154
 copyright, 149, 154
 limited, 32, 148
 patent, 32
  E.E.C., 33
 trade mark, 87
 unlawful conditions, 32, 33
LITERARY AGENTS, 160
LITERARY WORK. *See* WORKS, literary.

MANUSCRIPT,
 recipient's duties, 157, 160
MARK, 68 *et seq.*, 93, 96
MARKING,
 copyright notice, with, 117
MEDICINES, PATENTS FOR, 21, 45
MONOPOLY,
 abuse of, 86
 width of, 17 *et seq.*, 34
 And see WIDTH OF MONOPOLY.
MUSICAL WORKS, 125, 135, 137
 adaptation, 140, 144
 film music, 135, 158
 performance, 135, 140, 158
 recording of, 135, 141, 144, 154, 158

Index

NEWSPAPER REPORTS, 150
NOVELTY,
    invention, of, 11, 22, 26

OBTAINING OF INVENTION, 26
OBVIOUSNESS OF INVENTION, 18, 22, 26
OLD WORKS, 115
OPPOSITION,
    patent, to, 27
    trade mark registration, to, 75 et seq.
OWN NAME, USE OF, 65, 99
OWNER OF COPYRIGHT, 126 et seq.
    author, when not, 127
    commissioned works, 127, 156
    photographs, 127–128
    presumptions, 129
    recordings, 127

PARALLEL IMPORTS, 86
PASSING-OFF, 55 et seq., 97 et seq.
    company name, by, 57, 99, 103
PATENT. *See also* APPLICATION; INFRINGEMENT OF PATENT.
    addition, of, 47
    British, 16
    certificate of contested validity, 41
    chemical compound, for, 21, 45
    choice of, 17
    cost of, 17
    " designing round," 11, 30, 43
    duration, 13
    effectiveness, 6, 11 et seq., 30 et seq., 34, 41
    European, 16, 33, 36
        effect of, 17
    extension, 47
    fees, 22, 23, 24
    foreign, 36
    grant of, 23, 25
    improvement, for, 43
    infringement of. *See* INFRINGEMENT OF PATENT.
    invalidity, grounds of, 25–27
    licence, 32, 86, 170
    medicines, for, 21, 45–47
    opposition to, 27
    ownership of, 25
    period of protection, 24
    " prior grant," 27
    priority, 20, 22, 36
    protection, period of, 24
    revocation of, 24

PATENT—*cont.*
    secret, 54
    specification, 18, 35, *and see* PATENT SPECIFICATION.
    width of monopoly, 17 et seq., 34
PATENT AGENT, 21, 25, 38
PATENT APPLICATION,
    Convention, 36
    delay, 22
    examination, 21, 22, 23, 38
    foreign, 36 et seq.
    procedure, old, 27
    search, 21
PATENT OFFICE,
    appeals from. *See* APPEALS FROM PATENT OFFICE.
    European, 16
    " hearing " at, 24, 74
PATENT SPECIFICATION, 18, 35
    amendment of, 26
    " best method," 27
    claims, 18
    informal, 35
    instructions, 19
    insufficiency of, 26
PATENTED ARTICLE,
    dealings with, 32–33
    name of, as trade mark, 89
PATENTS COURT, 23
PERFORMANCE IN PUBLIC, 140
    broadcasting and, 141
    infringement of copyright by, 140
    musical works, 135, 141, 158
    permitting, 142, 144
    recordings, 146, 150
PERFORMING RIGHT, 158
    Society, 158
    Tribunal, 159
PERMISSION TO USE TRADE MARK, 83, 86 et seq.
PHOTOGRAPHS, 112, 118, 127, 145
    " author," 127
    building of, 151
    owner of copyright, 127, 128
    period of copyright, 145
    reproduction, 112, 137
PLACE NAMES AS TRADE MARKS, 69
PRICE CUTTING, 148
PRIOR PATENT GRANT, 27
PRIOR PUBLICATION, 26
PRIOR USE, 26
PRIORITY,
    patents, 20
    trade marks, 65, 91

176

Index

PRIVATE STUDY OF WORK, 149
PROSECUTION,
  Trade Descriptions Act, 4, 59, 108
PUBLIC PERFORMANCE. *See* PERFORMANCE IN PUBLIC.
PUBLICATION OF WORK,
  artistic works, 144
  definition, 144
  infringement by, 140, 144 *et seq.*
PUBLISHING AGREEMENTS, 157, 159

RECORDS AND RECORDINGS, 118, 125, 128, 146
  author, 127
  broadcasts from, 147
  duration of copyright, 146
  musical works, 135, 141, 145, 154, 159
  owner of copyright, 127
  performance, 146, 150
REGISTERED DESIGNS, 2, 12, 14, 52
REGISTERED USER OF MARK, 73, 87
REGISTRATION OF TRADE MARK. *See also* APPLICATION.
  " A," 57, 68, 95
  " B," 57 *et seq.*, 67, 74, 81 82
  company name, 70
  defensive, 80, 98
  false trade descriptions and, 110
  fees, 71
  goods, specification of, 60, 61, 71, 91
  opposition to, 74, 75
  validity, 60
REMOVAL OF MARK FROM REGISTER, 52, 79. *See* VALIDITY, Trade Mark Registration of.
REPRODUCTION OF WORK, 115, 132 *et seq.*, 144 *et seq.*
  adaptations, 139
  author, by, 128, 150
RESEARCH, USE OF WORK IN, 149
REVIEW OF WORK, 149
ROYALTIES,
  damages and, 9
  taxation, 44

SALE OF PATENT, 25
SCULPTURE, 50, 117, 144, 151
SEALING OF PATENT, 24

SECRECY, 29, 54
  See also CONFIDENTIAL INFORMATION.
SERIES OF MARKS, 72, 75
SEVEN YEAR OLD " A " MARKS, 79
SIGNATURE AS TRADE MARK, 70
SKETCHES FOR ARTISTIC WORK, 150
SLANDER OF GOODS, 105 *et seq.*
SPECIFICATION, *see* PATENT SPECIFICATION.
SUBSTANTIAL PART OF WORK, 134 *et seq.*
SURNAME AS TRADE MARK, 70, 99
SWIZZLESTICKS, 164

TAX. *See* INCOME TAX.
THREATS ACTION, 42, 47
TITLE,
  copyright in, 126
TRADE, CONNECTIONS IN COURSE OF, 68, 83
TRADE MARK. *See also* APPLICATION; " A "; " B "
  accessories, for, 64, 72
  assignment, 84
  associated, 76, 90
  certificate of contested validity, 66
  certification, 94 *et seq.*, 111
  chemical compounds, for, 89
  colours, 62
  copyright in, 113
  descriptive, 69, 79, 88
  design as, 69
  distinctiveness of, 69–71
  false, 105 *et seq.*
  foreign, 91
  foreign law, 82, 83, 85
  infringement of. *See* INFRINGEMENT OF TRADE MARK.
  initials as, 70
  invented word as, 69, 80, 90, 110
  joint ownership, 73
  licence, 83, 86 *et seq.*
  name, use of, 102
  patented article's name as, 89
  permission to use, 83, 87
  place names as, 69
  priority, 65, 91
  registered user of, 72, 73, 87
  registrability, 68, 71
  registration. *See* REGISTRATION OF TRADE MARK.
  removal of from register, 52, 79

177

Index

TRADE MARK—*cont.*
  series of, 72, 75
  seven year old " A " Marks, 79
  signature as, 70
  surname as, 70, 99
  unregistered, 84
  unused, 89
TRADE MARK AGENT, 71
TRADE MARK APPLICATION,
  advertisement of, 74
TRADE NAMES, 57, 97, 99
TRANSLATIONS, 124, 136
TYPOGRAPHICAL COPYRIGHT, 146

UNREGISTERED TRADE MARK, 84
UNUSED TRADE MARKS, 89
USE, PRIOR, 26
UTILITY OF INVENTION, 27

VALIDITY,
  contested, certificate of. *See* CERTIFICATE.
  grounds of patent invalidity, 25 *et seq.*
  trade mark registration, 60, 64, 66, 73, 80, 83 *et seq.*

WIDTH OF MONOPOLY,
  patent, 17 *et seq.*, 34
WORKS, 117 *et seq.*, 144 *et seq.*
  adaptations, 139
  anonymous, 125, 131
  architectural, 117, 128, 151

WORKS—*cont.*
  artistic, 49, 113, 125, 141, 144
  artistic craftsmanship, 50, 118
  classification, 115, 144 *et seq.*
  collective, 120, 124
  commissioned, 127–129, 156
  compilations, 123, 135
  craftsmanship, artistic, 50, 118
  dramatic, 117, 122, 139, 140, 144
  films, 139, 145
  indecent, 123
  infringing. *See* INFRINGING WORKS.
  literary, 113, 121–125, 138, 144
  merit, 117, 134
  musical, 125, 135, 137, 144, 154, 158
  old works, 115
  photographs, 112, 118, 127, 145
  private study of, 149
  publication of. *See* PUBLICATION OF WORK.
  quantum, 119, 120
  recordings, 118, 125, 128, 146, 154
  reproduction of. *See* REPRODUCTION OF WORK.
  research in, 149
  review of, 149
  sculpture, 50, 117, 144, 151
  substantial part of, 132 *et seq.*
  translation, 124, 136
  typographical arrangement, 146